MW00997723

Teaching Self-Discipline

The Responsive Classroom®
Guide to Helping Students
Dream, Behave, and Achieve
in Elementary School

—— FROM ——
RESPONSIVE CLASSROOM®

with Laurie Badge • Suzy Ghosh • Earl Hunter II

Caitie Meehan • Cory Wade

All net proceeds from the sale of this book support the work of Center for Responsive Schools, Inc., a not-for-profit educational organization and the developer of the *Responsive Classroom*® approach to teaching.

Many of the stories in this book are based on real events. To respect students' privacy, names and identifying characteristics of the students and situations have been changed.

© 2018 by Center for Responsive Schools, Inc.

All rights reserved. No part of this book may be reproduced in any form or by any electronic or mechanical means, including information storage and retrieval systems, without permission in writing from the publisher, except by a reviewer, who may quote brief passages in a review.

ISBN: 978-1-892989-91-8
Library of Congress Control Number: 2018938700

Classroom photographs by Jeff Woodward

Center for Responsive Schools, Inc.
85 Avenue A, P.O. Box 718
Turners Falls, MA 01376-0718

800-360-6332
www.responsiveclassroom.org

Second printing 2019

CONTENTS

Overview of the *Responsive Classroom*® Approach to Discipline

I magine a group of students sitting at a table together, everyone working on their history projects. Ethan sees that Chloe is using the stencil he wants, and she just went across the room to get some markers. Ethan could simply take the stencil, but he knows that in this classroom, the rule is to respect people's things. He also knows how important it is to be kind, and he doesn't want to make Chloe feel angry or upset. So, he waits until she returns to the table and asks, "Could I please use the stencil when you're done with it?" Everyone gets what they need, and class goes on productively.

When students develop internal motivation to do what's right, everyone benefits: the students, the teacher, and the entire classroom community. In contrast, when students have only external motivations shaping their behavior—earning a prize or a teacher's praise, or trying to avoid getting in trouble—it doesn't do much to help children develop self-discipline, ethical thinking, or an understanding of their roles as members of society. At its worst, such an approach invites tension, unquestioning obedience, or a constant battle of wills between adults and children in school.

This book offers a different approach to classroom discipline. It's an approach that has helped teachers in a wide range of elementary school settings establish calm and safe classrooms while helping children develop self-discipline and a sense of responsibility. It reflects the beliefs that discipline is a subject that can be taught, just as we teach reading and writing and math, and that children learn best when they're actively engaged and invested in constructing their own understanding.

This is not a new style of discipline. Since 1981, thousands of teachers have used it as part of the *Responsive Classroom* approach to teaching. The primary goals of this type of discipline are to:

1 Be kind yet firm so that students feel respected and encouraged

2 Build and maintain feelings of belonging and significance

3 Be effective in the long term at helping children control their behavior

4 Teach social and emotional skills

5 Help students use their personal power in positive ways

In classrooms using this approach to discipline, teachers take time to discuss students' goals for social and academic learning and how the rules can help everyone in class meet their goals. While there will always be times when students don't like following the rules or choose not to follow them, students in these schools generally view rules in a positive light.

As one third grader so clearly put it, "Rules in school are good because they help keep kids safe and in control so they can learn. But I'm glad at my school there isn't too many rules. Just a few good ones."

Voices in This Book

Throughout this book, you'll find examples of the *Responsive Classroom* approach in action at various grade levels. These examples come from real classrooms where teachers have seen the positive results of this approach, and can help you visualize how you might use the techniques outlined in this book in your own classroom.

Laurie Badge is a kindergarten teacher at Cedar Trails Elementary in Cedar Springs, Michigan. In her 31 years in the classroom, she has also taught third grade and kindergarten/first grade music. She has been practicing *Responsive Classroom* techniques for years and recently became a certified *Responsive Classroom* teacher.

Suzy Ghosh is a second grade teacher at Bush Hill Elementary School in Alexandria, Virginia. She has been using the *Responsive Classroom* approach in her classroom for the last 10 years. She also teaches the approach as a *Responsive Classroom* consulting teacher.

Earl Hunter II is a fifth grade teacher at Oakwood Elementary School in North Hollywood, California, where he is enjoying his 19th year of teaching. In his words, Mr. Hunter has been enlightened by sharing the *Responsive Classroom* approach for over 10 of those years.

Caitie Meehan is a fourth grade math teacher at School Within School @ Goding in Washington, DC, where she helps students build math confidence. She has been practicing and teaching the *Responsive Classroom* approach for almost 10 years.

Cory Wade is a third grade teacher at Hillcrest Community School in Bloomington, Minnesota, and is in his 13th year of teaching. He has been practicing the *Responsive Classroom* approach for almost 11 years and presenting the *Responsive Classroom* Course and Advanced Course to educators all over the world for the past six years.

Common Styles of Teacher Leadership

As teachers, our approach to discipline is influenced by our own experiences as students, our teacher-education background, and many other factors. We may stick with what we knew as children, or we may push against it with a radically different disciplinary style. No matter what the approach, there's a good chance it fits into one of the following leadership styles.

An Autocratic Style: *"Because I said so!"*

The autocratic style often features a long list of rules, generally stated in the negative, presented without discussion, and focused on being quiet and obedient. For many of us, this is the teaching style we experienced as children. Therefore, it can feel intuitive to teach this way ourselves. The underlying belief behind this style of leadership is that children are by nature unruly and impulsive—largely incapable of self-regulation—and it's our responsibility to make them behave. Without the rules, students' natural impulses will take hold and at any moment, chaos will erupt: thirty children racing around the classroom, screaming at the top of their lungs, gum dropping from their mouths, everyone pushing and fighting with one another.

An autocratic style doesn't focus on whether or not students understand the rules, only on whether or not they follow them. Many children do opt to comply in this type of system, but largely out of fear of what will happen to them if they don't. Others become masterful at putting on a good show for the teacher while completely disregarding the rules when no one's looking. Still others become defiant or, at the other extreme, so completely dependent on adults to guide their behavior that they find it impossible to make ethical decisions on their own.

This approach can achieve an orderly classroom, but at what cost? A leadership style that's based on fear and punishment externally controls children but does little to teach them self-control. It achieves compliance, but it also yields anxiety, resentment, and anger. While the classroom might appear calm and productive on the outside, students often feel humiliated, afraid, and resentful on the inside—hardly optimal conditions for learning.

A Permissive Style:
"Can you please cooperate now, please?"

On the other end of the spectrum is a permissive approach to rules and discipline in which there are no clear limits for behavior. Here, rules are negotiable and easily bendable. They may be clearly stated and posted in a prominent place in the room, but everyone knows they won't be enforced consistently.

Teachers using this leadership style may believe that the most important thing is for children to like them. They may put a high premium on being nice and may worry about stifling or alienating their students by being too hard on them. Or, they might believe that the best way to influence children's behavior is to ignore undesirable actions while reinforcing desirable ones with generous doses of praise. Or, perhaps, they've experienced the negative effects of an autocratic approach and don't want to inflict it on others.

Whatever the underlying intention, a permissive style leads to many problems. Among them, small disturbances routinely escalate into bigger ones, conflicts are unresolved, and rudeness, teasing, and taunting go unchecked, leaving many children feeling physically and psychologically unsafe. If, somehow, students are behaving in such a classroom, they're often doing so only to please the teacher and win their approval.

Without a reliable structure and firm boundaries, students in these classrooms can feel just as fearful, tense, and dependent as those in classrooms using an autocratic approach. It may seem counterintuitive, but having too much freedom can actually make children feel anxious rather than free as they try to figure out where the limits are and how they're supposed to behave.

Teachers hold so little authority in these classrooms that when they do need to gain control, they often resort to pleading, cajoling, or bribing to try and convince students to cooperate. These teachers may grow so discouraged by students' behavior and the lack of cooperation that they end up feeling burnt out.

A Flip-Flop Style: *"I said 'No.' Well, maybe one more chance. Now, that's it. I mean 'No.'"*

There are teachers, many of them in their early years of teaching and without much support around classroom management, who bounce back and forth between the autocratic and permissive extremes. This kind of discipline can cause confusion, frustration, and anxiety for students and teachers alike due to its complete lack of predictability and consistency.

Although new teachers may have learned about classroom management in teacher-education coursework, actually managing 25 or more students in a small space for seven hours a day can be challenging, especially if teachers lack mentoring or administrative support. But it's not only new teachers who face this challenge. Experienced teachers, too, can feel overwhelmed by the demands placed on them as more and more students come to school with poorly developed social skills, a lack of impulse control, and few tools to handle their anger and frustration.

Discipline in our nation's classrooms and schools is clearly a pressing concern and an important factor in students' success. How teachers approach discipline can make all the difference between whether children feel safe or threatened in school, motivated or discouraged, successful or defeated.

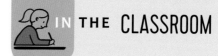

IN THE CLASSROOM

Leadership Styles

Throughout this book, you'll get real-world advice and points of view from teachers experienced in using the *Responsive Classroom* approach. See page 3 to meet them!

Ms. Meehan, Grade 4 ● Before she discovered the *Responsive Classroom* style of leadership, Ms. Meehan felt like she was always bribing and manipulating her students to get them to behave. That meant a lot more work for her, with daily behavior reports, color charts, prizes, and everything else she had to keep track of. The approach didn't work well in the long run for students, either. Holding up one student as a good example harmed that student's image with their classmates, and students who consistently didn't win prizes felt little incentive to try and behave well.

Ms. Ghosh, Grade 2 ● In Ms. Ghosh's first few years of teaching, she used a stoplight system to monitor behavior. Each student had their name on a clothespin that she moved from green to yellow to red—a system she didn't like, but she wasn't sure what else to do. She found she wasn't consistent in which behaviors got a student moved to the next color, and if a student was on red by 9:30 in the morning, they often got frustrated, feeling like they couldn't do anything right and had no incentive to behave well for the rest of the day. She finally dropped the system because it didn't make any sense to her and didn't help the students learn self-control.

The *Responsive Classroom* Style of Teacher Leadership

The leadership style described in this book is neither autocratic nor permissive, but authoritative. It is respectful, encouraging, and kind, yet firm. It comes from a place of empathy for students, and is firmly rooted in the belief that children want to do what's right. The *Responsive Classroom* style of leadership aims to help children develop self-control, learn about what socially responsible behavior is, and come to value such behavior.

The approach to discipline that comes out of this leadership style does not rely on punishment or rewards to "get students to behave." Neither does it ignore behavior that is detrimental to the child or to the group. Rather, this approach offers clear expectations for behavior and actively teaches children how to live up to those expectations.

Using this approach helps children become aware of how their actions can bring positive and negative consequences to themselves and others. When children misbehave, respectful strategies help stop the misbehavior and restore positive behavior as quickly as possible so that children can continue to learn and we can continue to teach.

> This approach offers clear expectations for behavior and actively teaches children how to live up to those expectations.

In an authoritative leadership style, teachers strive to be firm, kind, and consistent. Our aim is to create calm, safe, and orderly classrooms while preserving the dignity of each child. This requires a constant balancing of the needs of the group with the needs of the individual, the need for order with the need for movement and activity, the need for teachers to be in control of the classroom with the need for students to be in control of their own lives and learning. It requires taking the time to teach children how to be contributing members of a caring learning community.

Just as we don't expect children to come to school knowing how to read and write, teachers using this approach don't make assumptions about how advanced children's social skills are when they arrive in the classroom. Some children will come to school with highly developed social skills and many years of experience being part of a large group. Others will need to start from the beginning.

School is rich with opportunities for children to learn to think and act in socially responsible ways.

School provides an ideal setting for social learning. There are endless opportunities at school for children to learn to control their impulses and to think about the needs and feelings of others. Whether they're learning to wait their turn to talk, ask politely for a marker, welcome a newcomer into a group, or respectfully discuss topics from a variety of viewpoints, school is rich with opportunities for children to learn to think and act in socially responsible ways.

The *Responsive Classroom* Discipline Framework

In the chapters that follow, you'll learn practical strategies for establishing clear behavior expectations and teaching students how to meet these expectations. You will also learn tools and techniques for how to respond effectively when children misbehave.

The *Responsive Classroom* approach to discipline is built on the understanding that in order to be successful in and out of school, students need to learn specific social and emotional competencies. These competencies are as follows:

- **Cooperation:** Students' ability to establish new relationships, maintain positive relationships and friendships, avoid social isolation, resolve conflicts, accept differences, be contributing members of the classroom and school community, and work productively and collaboratively with others

- **Assertiveness:** Students' ability to take initiative, stand up for their ideas without hurting or negating others, seek help, succeed at challenging tasks, and recognize their individual selves as separate from the circumstances or conditions they're in

- **Responsibility:** Students' ability to motivate themselves to take action and follow through on expectations; to define a problem, consider the consequences, and choose a positive solution

- **Empathy:** Students' ability to recognize and understand another's state of mind and emotions and be receptive to new ideas and perspectives; to appreciate and value differences and diversity in others; to have concern for others' welfare, even when it doesn't benefit or may come at a cost to one's self

- **Self-Control:** Students' ability to recognize and regulate their thoughts, emotions, and behaviors in order to be successful in the moment and remain on a successful trajectory

All of the information in this book is based on the *Responsive Classroom* discipline framework, which maps to these five competencies. This framework includes five key components, each with a set of goals for teachers.

Responsive Classroom Discipline Framework

Component	Goals
Creating a safe and predictable learning environment	To lay the foundation for a safe and positive learning community
Preventing off-task behavior and misbehavior	To establish rules and hold students to those rules in a proactive, firm, fair, and consistent manner
Responding to off-task behavior and misbehavior	To handle off-task behavior and misbehavior respectfully, and to help the student get back on task, repair any damage caused, and develop self-discipline so as to prevent similar problems in the future
Solving chronic behavior problems	To understand the student's particular behavior problem and address it with modified or individualized discipline practices that help the student develop self-regulation; to help the student learn which strategies for returning to positive behavior work for them
Managing outbursts	To deescalate or interrupt behavioral or emotional outbursts, and to draw on community support to help a student regain self-control at the point of escalation

Mirroring this framework, the first two chapters of this book focus on how to build a solid foundation for positive behavior by creating a safe learning environment and investing students in the rules.

Chapter 3 explains how to help students get back on task when they lose track of the rules and misbehave, as all students will at some point.

Finally, the last two chapters help you address more challenging behavior problems, including those that may be the result of toxic stress.

Through the use of this framework and the techniques outlined in this book, you can foster the essential social and emotional learning competencies students need and create learning environments where they can thrive. The skills students learn now will serve them in their lives both inside and outside the classroom, in the present and for a lifetime.

Reflecting on One's Own Social and Emotional Skills

How well children are able to control their behavior has a lot to do with their still-developing social and emotional skills. In order to support students' social and emotional learning, it's essential to reflect on and develop those skills in ourselves as teachers.

The Collaborative for Academic, Social, and Emotional Learning (n.d.) highlights five core social-emotional competencies, which can be taught in a variety of ways. One essential way to teach these competencies is by modeling them so that students can see them in action.

These five competencies are:

- **Self-awareness**—recognizing one's own thoughts, emotions, strengths, and limitations, and understanding how they influence one's behavior

- **Self-management**—regulating one's emotions and behaviors, including managing stress, controlling impulses, and motivating oneself to work toward goals

- **Social awareness**—empathizing with people from different backgrounds and understanding social and ethical norms for behavior

- **Relationship skills**—establishing and maintaining healthy relationships with individuals and groups through clear communication, cooperation, resisting peer pressure, and conflict resolution

- **Responsible decision-making**—making constructive choices about behavior and social interactions, considering the well-being of oneself and others, and evaluating the consequences of one's actions

Reference

Collaborative for Academic, Social, and Emotional Learning. n.d. "Core SEL Competencies." Accessed July 6, 2018. https://casel.org/core-competencies/.

Creating a Safe and Predictable Learning Environment

Creating a Safe and Predictable Learning Environment

I t's the first day of school. Walking into their new classrooms, students have a million questions: Will my new teacher be nice? What do I do if I need to go to the bathroom? Will the other kids be friendly? Do I have to stay at my desk? Will there be a lot of homework?

Everyone needs this kind of information in new situations. Whether walking into a new job, a new social group, or a new country, we as social beings need to know the customs and codes of conduct in any new environment. Children, especially, crave this kind of information, and they need it during the first few days of school in order to feel safe and ready to learn.

From day one, we need to convey the message that in this classroom, respect, kindness, and learning will prevail. Students need to know with certainty that the teacher is in control and that the standards for behavior are high. This knowledge gives students a sense of physical and emotional security and frees them to participate in all classroom activities in a meaningful way.

The tools and advice in this chapter can help you build the foundation for a safe and productive learning environment. The ways in which these techniques are implemented will vary according to children's developmental level and experience with procedures and routines from other grades, but children of all ages will benefit from time spent establishing order from the first day of school.

To learn more about children's development and how it affects them in the classroom, see *Yardsticks: Child and Adolescent Development Ages 4–14* by Chip Wood (Center for Responsive Schools, 2017).

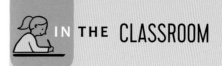

IN THE CLASSROOM

The Beginning of the School Year

Mrs. Badge, Grade K ● In the past, Mrs. Badge used to jump in and start assessing children's skills on day one, but now she takes the opposite approach, starting in as slow and relaxed a manner as possible. Having a calm and inviting attitude on the first day lets kindergartners know that everything will be okay and that they can handle school. Mrs. Badge starts off with a simple Morning Meeting, talking about what it means to be a family, and how the classroom is a family, too, where everyone will treat others with kindness and listen to each other.

Mr. Wade, Grade 3 ● From the beginning of the year, Mr. Wade always refers to "our classroom" to build students' sense of ownership. He wants the classroom to feel like home for the students in his class and to be a place where people help each other. For example, students who arrive early for the before-school program have already had a chance to get to know the general layout of the room, so he enlists their help to support others—particularly students who are new to the school and need a bit of extra assistance.

Ms. Meehan, Grade 4 ● A warm and inviting morning message lets students know they'll have a chance to get to know each other and their teacher before diving fully into academics. Ms. Meehan emphasizes the importance of using a calm, friendly tone of voice in the early days of school, especially when redirecting students and correcting mistakes. She also keeps a pad of sticky notes on her desk so students can write down their questions, which she answers at appropriate times during the first few weeks of school. This helps clarify expectations and reduce students' anxieties about the new year.

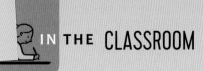

The Beginning of the School Year

Ms. Ghosh, Grade 2 ● Ms. Ghosh helps students acclimate at the beginning of the year by frequently talking about how they'll do things in second grade. Saying things like "This is how we'll put our backpacks away in second grade" acknowledges that procedures and routines may be a little different than they were in first grade. It also helps often perfectionistic new second graders (who may still be attached to their first grade teachers) know that the way they're doing things now isn't wrong—it's just new.

Mr. Hunter, Grade 5 ● Mr. Hunter sets expectations right from the start on the first day of school. He gives each student a friendly greeting as they enter the room, but doesn't do much talking once they're in and getting settled that first day. This demonstrates to students that they need to take responsibility for reading the directions he puts up on the board—and that he believes in their capacity to do so.

Before School Starts

Mrs. Badge, Grade K ● At the open house just before school starts, Mrs. Badge makes it fun for new students to get acclimated to the classroom. She sets up a scavenger hunt for children and parents to do together to find their cubby, their table assignment, the water fountain, the bathroom, and other essentials. She also helps children practice the basic skills they'll need for the first day, like hanging up their coats. If any families don't come to the open house, she calls them right away to try and schedule a visit. Having most students in the class know the basic layout and routine really helps things run smoothly on the first day of school.

Picture a student walking into a new classroom on the first day of school, and imagine it through their eyes.

Organizing the Classroom for Success

Picture a student walking into a new classroom on the first day of school, and imagine it through their eyes. Does the room look organized or chaotic? Does it seem to have space for them and their work, or is it packed full of displays and materials they don't know about yet? Most importantly, does it seem like a place that is safe and welcoming, one that will encourage them to learn, grow, make new friends, and be creative?

The ideal classroom is one that is organized with purpose, featuring plenty of room for students' work on the walls, developmentally appropriate furniture and supplies, and spaces to learn individually and in small and large groups. Here are some tips for setting up a classroom where students can feel at home, understand and follow expectations, and be ready to start learning from day one.

Furniture—To set the stage for collaborative work, consider arranging tables or desk clusters to allow students to sit in small groups. Assigning seats on the first day may relieve anxiety, and designating a color, animal, or shape for each table or cluster can provide a quick way to help students regroup and identify themselves. Each table or cluster can have its own supply of materials to make and decorate name tags, an ideal activity for getting to know each other on the first day of school.

**Bulletin Board Title Ideas
for the First Day**

• Hopes and Dreams for the Year

• Birthday Chart

• Favorite Books and Authors

• All About Us

• Word Wall (include a few words
  to start)

Classroom walls—Walls covered with all sorts of displays can lead students to feel overwhelmed, but bare walls and boards look too bleak. One way to strike a balance—displaying just enough to pique students' curiosity—is to keep most wall space or bulletin boards blank, but give them bold titles and attractive frames. The framed, open spaces serve as a sign that you and your students will build your classroom displays together.

A circle area—A space where students can come together in one circle makes for a safe gathering spot for class discussions, mini-lessons, and activities—where all voices are heard, all people are valued, and everyone can see and be seen. As you plan for seating in the circle, consider the developmental needs of your students. Fifth graders' bigger bodies might call for chairs, while first or second graders, who are prone to falling out of chairs, may be better off on the floor. You might also consider assigning places in the circle if needed to prevent competitiveness or break up cliques. No matter what seating arrangements you choose, students and adults in the circle should be able to see one another easily. Keep the circle open in the middle, but have a chart stand or whiteboard accessible for writing messages and listing ideas. In some classrooms, students may need to carry their chairs to the circle area or move desks to create space, so these procedures should be taught early through Interactive Modeling (see pages 28-31).

Classroom supplies—Consider keeping supplies out of reach or clearly marked as off limits until it's time to introduce them and teach students how to use them appropriately. For materials that won't be used until later in the year, it might make sense to tuck them away in a closet or supply cabinet to keep them out of sight. Materials that will be used early and often—but not right away—might be kept in bins or on shelves with signs that say "Coming Attraction!" in order to let students know these are for use soon and to build excitement. Mr. Wade puts out old crayons on day one so his third graders will be able to color in name tags and do other early activities before he teaches them the proper use of newer supplies later on.

For more information about setting up your classroom, see the *What Every Teacher Needs to Know* series for grades K–5 by Margaret Berry Wilson and Mike Anderson (Center for Responsive Schools, 2010–2011).

Before School Starts

Mr. Hunter, Grade 5 ● Early spring is "recruiting time" for Mr. Hunter. Like a college sports recruiter scouting out high school games, he observes the fourth grade classrooms in his school to see students in action. He creates a mental list of the cast of characters he'll be seeing in the fall, such as the students who show strong leadership skills so that he can enlist them as allies in building community. This practice also helps him understand the classroom culture his students are coming from so that he can help them transition as the new school year begins.

Mr. Wade, Grade 3 ● Mr. Wade takes the opportunity to learn as much as he can from students' records before they enter his classroom. Do they have any medical issues he needs to be aware of? How have they done on testing? Whom do they live with? He goes through this information, looking for the positive and beginning to get a sense of each student as a whole child. After that, he observes students at back-to-school night to learn more. Which students already know each other, and who might benefit from sitting near (or away from) a particular student or group? How are students' writing and number skills when they write their names and birthdays on the birthday chart? These observations will give him a head start on day one in building relationships with his students.

Using Positive Teacher Language

Research has shown that children's academic performance is influenced both positively and negatively by teachers' expectations. If a teacher believes a child will succeed, the child has a greater chance of doing so than if the teacher believes the child will fail. The same holds true for children's behavior.

Teacher language is one key way of communicating our expectations to children. It can demonstrate confidence in students' ability to meet high expectations—and it can recognize their efforts at behaving well. Positive teacher language encourages and supports students, rather than criticizing them for their mistakes.

> If a teacher believes a child will succeed, the child has a greater chance of doing so than if the teacher believes the child will fail.

Effective teacher language can be used to help students visualize positive outcomes for themselves, to recognize their efforts, and to help them get back on task when they make mistakes. No matter the purpose, effective teacher language:

- Is clear, simple, and direct
- Is genuine and respectful
- Gives specific positive feedback rather than general praise
- Focuses on the child's action or behavior rather than generalizing about the child's whole person
- Avoids qualitative or personal judgment
- Shows faith in children's ability to follow the rules

Envisioning language offers a view of what students are capable of achieving. It helps them see what the goal is, picture themselves achieving it, and believe in their own ability to do so. By using envisioning language to name positive identities for students, we help them form a vision of themselves as learners. To use envisioning language effectively:

- **Think about positive identities for students.** Referring to them as "readers," "writers," "scientists," "athletes," "teammates," "artists," or "musicians" can generate excitement and help students identify as successful learners.

mathematicians

- **Use concrete words and images that children understand instead of abstract terms.** Instead of telling students they need to be respectful listeners during an upcoming assembly, you might talk about having quiet mouths and eyes on the speaker so everyone can enjoy the presentation.

- **Use metaphors to add clarity and power.** These metaphors can come from the curriculum, classroom life, or your own experiences. For example, if your class has been learning about the American Revolution, you might say, "Today, you're going to declare your independence by choosing your own books to read from our library!"

Examples of Envisioning Language

"Geology is the science of our planet's history. Today, we'll all be geologists as we examine rocks from around our school."

"Today, you're going to write stories that help readers see, smell, and hear what's going on."

"Our classroom is like an orchestra. We all have our own unique parts to play, but when we listen to each other and work together, we can create beautiful music!"

Reinforcing language names and affirms children's positive behaviors. Recognizing that children build on their strengths, we use reinforcing language to help children know exactly what they are doing well and to help them grow academically and socially. To use reinforcing language effectively:

- **Name concrete, specific behaviors and emphasize description over personal approval.** For example, "Did you notice how quickly everyone cleaned up today?" is more effective than "I liked how you all cleaned up so quickly." The goal is to help children learn to self-assess and to increase their internal sense of self-worth rather than always looking to the teacher for validation. Specific encouragement ("The illustrations in your science report were so detailed!") helps children understand what they're doing well so that they can build on it. General praise ("Great job on your science report!"), on the other hand, only provides external validation on which students may become dependent, which can keep them from building their own self-confidence.

- **Find positives to name in all students.** It's important that reinforcing language be used authentically with all children, not just those who excel. Observe children carefully and acknowledge the small but important steps they take toward mastery of a skill or behavior.

Examples of Reinforcing Language

"Today, you got started on your work right away. That means you will have time to start publishing your work this afternoon."

"You used lots of descriptive language in your story about the visit to the farm. I got a clear picture of all the animals you saw."

"Jamil, you listened so carefully and attentively during sharing. Your questions and comments showed that you were really paying attention to the speaker."

- **Direct reinforcing language only toward the student being reinforced.** Give reinforcement privately, unless it is genuinely directed at the entire group. While it can be tempting to hold one student's exemplary behavior up as a model for others ("Look how well Jacob cleaned up his desk area!"), there are risks in doing so. The individual student might feel manipulated or distrustful of your positive feedback, and their classmates might feel resentful of the student being praised. It's best to find more direct ways of letting students know what your expectations are.

- **Be sincere.** While there may be a period of time when your language sounds a bit unnatural because of changes you're trying to make in how you talk with children, it's important to always maintain your sincerity. Students know when your language is coming from a genuine place and when it's not.

IN THE CLASSROOM

Teacher Language on Day One

Mr. Wade, Grade 3 • On the first day, when students are just beginning to learn the classroom expectations, teacher language can be a powerful tool. Mr. Wade uses basic reminding language to keep students on task with directions he's given them: "Remind me what you should be doing right now." Envisioning language is also essential as he sets expectations for the year. If a student asks, "Why are we doing this?" he includes envisioning language when stating the goal: "The goal is that we're going to know each other really well." Many children are nervous on the first day of school, so Mr. Wade strives to keep a calm tone and reassure them when needed. Rather than putting words in their mouths ("You must be so excited for the first day of school!"), he asks what students are feeling so that they know their thoughts and feelings matter.

Reminding language prompts children to remember established expectations and to make decisions about their actions based on those expectations. It communicates our trust in students' good intentions. Unlike day-to-day "reminders" that are common in adult life (such as to pick up the dry cleaning or put out the garbage), reminding language puts the responsibility for doing the remembering on the child rather than the adult who is doing the reminding. Reminders can be either a question ("What are you supposed to be doing right now?") or a statement ("Show me how you should be doing this"), and can be used either to help children prepare for an activity or situation or to steady the course when students are beginning to go off task.

Here are a few tips for using reminding language effectively:

- **Establish expectations before using reminders.** In order to use reminders successfully, it's essential to teach and practice the procedures and behavior expectations that the reminders refer to.

- **Use a direct tone and neutral body language.** Tone and body language communicate a lot about a teacher's underlying beliefs. No matter how carefully we choose our words, if our tone and body language convey impatience, irritation, or judgment, the message will be that we don't really have faith in children's good intentions. One trick for keeping your tone neutral is to visualize the student doing the right thing before you speak. That way, you're aligning your underlying beliefs with a positive vision of the student.

- **Keep reminders simple and brief.** Using too many words confuses and overwhelms children, and after a certain point, they stop listening. If behavior expectations are clear, there's no need to go into a long explanation.

- **Pay attention to the small things.** The time to issue a reminder is when the off-task behavior is just beginning. Reminding students about using respectful indoor voices will have much more impact when the noise level is just starting to rise above a productive level than it will after the classroom has become raucous.

Examples of Reminding Language

Before students start on a project that requires them to share markers:
"Who can show us how to safely and politely pass a marker?"

A group of students begins to whisper and giggle instead of doing their math work:
"Show me what to do if you don't remember what you're supposed to be working on."

Before student presentations:
"One of our rules says to respect each other. What do we need to do to be a respectful audience?"

Redirecting language is used when a student's behavior needs to be stopped immediately. Unlike reminding language, which lets the student figure out what they need to do, redirecting language is used after the student has lost control and needs help getting back on task. We calmly and clearly tell the child to stop and explain exactly what to do instead. The goal is to stop the misbehavior quickly so that the child can regain control and positive behavior can be restored as soon as possible. Because it is non-negotiable, redirecting language is always given as a statement, never a question. Here are some other tips for using redirecting language effectively:

Examples of Redirecting Language

Suzanne throws the paintbrush across the table instead of handing it to Ramon:
"Suzanne, pick up the paintbrush and hand it to Ramon."

Jimmy taps and pokes his neighbors during a meeting:
"Jimmy, hands in your lap."

While working in small groups, several students start running around the classroom:
"Freeze. Voices off. Everyone go back to your tables."

- **Be firm when needed.** In an effort to avoid seeming mean, many teachers shy away from being firm. This does a great disservice to everyone. Students grow uncertain about limits, and we lose our authority to establish those limits. A simple guideline to keep in mind is: "If you mean no, then say no." No hedging, no beating around the bush.

- **Use direct statements.** Another way some teachers try to avoid seeming mean is by phrasing their instructions as questions. But because students who are misbehaving need help getting back in control, it's our job as teachers to give them the clear directions they need. Instead of asking, "Could you please put your brushes down and look at me?" say, "Put your brushes down and look at me."

- **Pay attention to tone and volume.** Most children are keenly aware of the subtle and not-so-subtle alterations in meaning caused by tone and volume. Watch out for the negative tone that slyly slips in or the raised volume that makes a directive sound more like a threat, instead striving for a calm, neutral tone and reasonable volume that match the intended message.

- **Keep it simple and clear.** Often, a single phrase or directive is all that's needed. It can be hard for students to follow a long lecture and understand it rationally when they're out of control. A quick redirection like "Hands to yourself" or "Freeze—scissors on the desk" is much more effective.

- **Sometimes, use humor.** You might give literally hundreds of reminders and redirections in the course of a normal school day. If you're beginning to feel like a broken record, it might be time to infuse some humor into the situation. For example, a teacher who steps into the hallway to speak to the principal for a minute returns to find the classroom noisy and chaotic. He turns off the light, signaling students to stop what they're doing and look at him, then says, "I'm going to perform a magic trick right now. When I say 'abracadabra,' everyone magically change back to focused learning mode!"

The process of changing one's language takes time and effort, and it starts with assessing where you are now. Listen consciously to your own words. You could also video- or audiorecord yourself in the classroom, or team up with a colleague to take turns observing each other for 15 minutes and recording the words you each use most frequently.

Once you've identified your own patterns, pick one to focus on changing. You can try working with one or more colleagues to make this change together, or even enlist students to remind you when you need help. When you do make a mistake, try fixing it in the moment. You might say something like "Rewind—what I meant to say was . . ." Not only will doing so help you change, but it will model for students how to be a learner who makes mistakes and works to fix them.

As you continue the process of changing your language, remember to pause before speaking to give yourself a chance to think. And give yourself reminders, too: Post a list of desirable words and phrases in your classroom for easy reference, or write them on a card that you can carry in your pocket or tape to the back of your ID badge. Finally, try relying more on nonverbal signals and cues as a way to get students' attention. This will reduce the amount of "teacher talk," allowing you to focus more fully on the most important language patterns.

Through all of this, remember that change takes time. Be patient with yourself and celebrate the incremental improvements you make along the way.

To learn more about using positive teacher language, see *The Power of Our Words: Teacher Language That Helps Children Learn* by Paula Denton (Center for Responsive Schools, 2013).

> Remember that change takes time. Be patient with yourself and celebrate the incremental improvements you make along the way.

Teaching and Modeling Procedures and Routines

Children are able, even eager, to rise to high standards of behavior, but they need to know exactly what those standards are. It's best not to assume that they know what's expected of them, even in the most routine situations. If we expect students to walk instead of run when moving around the room, put away materials after using them, share materials, raise their hand to speak, or show attention and interest when a classmate is talking, then we have to be clear and direct about these expectations.

Interactive Modeling is a powerful technique for breaking down and teaching many different behaviors, from classroom procedures to social skills.

When teaching new behaviors, it's essential to break them down into manageable parts and teach those parts individually. This is especially important in primary grades, when students are often learning procedures and routines for the first time. For example, the procedure of standing in line could be broken down into the following steps:

- Paying attention to the signal for quiet
- Moving to the line-up area safely and quietly
- Finding your place in line
- Standing quietly until the teacher gives further instructions

Interactive Modeling is a powerful technique for breaking down and teaching many different behaviors, from classroom procedures to social skills. Simple and direct, this technique is used to teach the nonnegotiable procedures and routines that help keep the classroom running smoothly and safely. Interactive Modeling allows students to observe, think about, and practice a new skill in order to effectively learn what a positive behavior looks like, sounds like, and feels like.

Steps of Interactive Modeling

1 **Say what you will model and why.** Be sure to state the behavior and goal in the positive. For example: "I'm going to show you how to carry scissors. That's going to help everybody stay safe and follow our rule to take care of ourselves and each other."

2 **Model the behavior.** Demonstrate the procedure exactly as you expect students to do it (the right way, not the wrong way, and without narrating what you're doing).

3 **Ask students what they noticed.** You may need to do some prompting, but children soon notice every little detail, especially as they gain expertise with this practice. If they include details phrased in the negative ("You didn't talk"), ask them what you did do instead ("You were quiet").

4 **Invite one or more students to model.** They should demonstrate the skill for the class in the same way you did.

5 **Again, ask students what they noticed.** This helps them reinforce what they saw you do and pick up on anything they might have missed the first time.

6 **Have all students practice.** Observe and coach the class while they model the behavior.

7 **Provide feedback.** Name specific, positive actions you notice, and redirect respectfully but clearly when students go off task.

In the following pages, you'll see examples of Interactive Modeling used during the early days of school at two grade levels, second grade and fifth grade.

A Second Grade Class Learns How to Listen Attentively

1 **The teacher says what he will model and why.** "Many times during our school day, we'll be listening to each other share ideas. It's important that we listen carefully so we can follow our rule to be kind to others."

2 **The teacher models the behavior.** The teacher has arranged ahead of time for Sharice to help with today's Interactive Modeling. Now he says to the class, "Sharice is going to talk about something that will be happening after school tomorrow. I'll be the listener. Notice what I do." Sharice makes an announcement about a dress rehearsal for a school play. The teacher listens attentively.

3 **The teacher asks students what they noticed.** He asks, "What did I do to show that I was listening?" Students respond, "You looked at her." "You looked like you were concentrating. You looked serious." One student says, "You didn't move around." The teacher asks, "What did I do instead?" "You kept your body still," the student replies.

4 **The teacher invites one or more students to model the behavior.** "Who else would like to show how to listen in a respectful way?" Mikaela and Tony raise their hands. "OK, this time Mikaela will be the speaker. She's going to tell Tony about a friend of hers who will be visiting tomorrow." The class watches Tony as Mikaela shares.

5 **The teacher again asks what students noticed.** Students say what they saw and heard. "You nodded your head." "You smiled when she told you how excited she was about her friend visiting."

6 **The whole class practices the behavior.** "Let's all practice attentive listening now," the teacher says. "I'll share something with you and you can all show how you listen."

7 **The teacher provides feedback.** "I saw students listening with closed mouths and their eyes on me. I saw students keeping their hands still in their laps. We're going to keep practicing this skill as the year goes on."

A Fifth Grade Class Learns How to Move Safely to the Circle Area

1 **The teacher says what she will model and why.** "When we move from the tables to the circle for Morning Meeting, we need to take care of each other by moving safely."

2 **The teacher models the behavior.** She knows that many students experienced Morning Meeting in fourth grade and know how to make a safe transition to the meeting circle, so she asks for ideas. "Let's say I'm doing my morning work and I hear the chime for Morning Meeting. What do I need to do?" The teacher then demonstrates using the students' suggestions.

3 **The teacher asks students what they noticed.** "What did you notice about how I moved to the meeting circle?" the teacher asks. Students answer, "You stood up carefully so that you didn't knock the chair over." "You walked to the circle." "You kept your hands to yourself."

4 **The teacher invites one or more students to model the behavior.** "Now we need one of you to show us how to move safely to the circle." Caitlyn volunteers. Her classmates watch and notice what she does.

5 **The teacher again asks what students noticed.** Students say what they saw and heard. "You set your chair down gently when you got to the circle." "You watched where you were going."

6 **The whole class practices the behavior.** "This week, when we move to the circle for Morning Meeting, let's all pay special attention to how we move safely," the teacher says. "We'll check in on Friday about how we're doing with this." In this example, the whole-class practice takes place in the days after the Interactive Modeling. This can be very effective as long as the teacher lets students know that she will be noticing their actions and the class gathers again to reflect on their practice.

7 **The teacher provides feedback.** After Friday's Morning Meeting, the teacher says, "I saw people moving chairs safely and making room for each other in the circle. We were able to get into the circle much more quickly today because of all that practice!"

After behaviors have been taught, it's helpful to occasionally remind students how to do them. You can borrow from the steps of Interactive Modeling to provide brief reminders that happen spontaneously throughout the day. For example, a first grade teacher rings the bell and tells students that it's time to put away reading materials and line up to go to lunch. She asks, "Who can remind us how to put away our reading materials in a safe and careful way?"

"You should walk," says one student.

"Put all the papers back in the folder neatly," says another.

A third student says, "Don't push people when you're in line to put your folder away."

"What should you do if you're not going to push people?" the teacher asks.

"Wait for your turn if someone's in front of you."

"Wow! You remember a lot about how to put our reading materials away in a safe and careful way," says the teacher. "Who would like to show us?"

> Children learn just as much—if not more—from their spontaneous interactions with us as they do from deliberate lessons.

Three children raise their hands. The rest of the students watch from their seats. The three children follow the suggestions given by the students. They put their papers away neatly in the folder, walk to the file cabinet, put their folders away, and line up at the door.

"What did you notice?" asks the teacher.

"Dwayne had to take all his papers out to get them in neatly."

"Thea waited for Helen to finish 'cause their files were right next to each other."

"They all walked. No one bumped into each other."

"It was really quiet."

The teacher nods and says, "It sounds like we're ready for everyone to give it a try. Go ahead and put away your reading materials and line up for lunch." Once the students have done so, the teacher reinforces their efforts. "I saw first graders putting their reading materials away carefully and safely and lining up for lunch. That helps us take care of our materials and each other!"

Interactive Modeling can also be fun. Anything involving acting is inherently fun for many children. Students enjoy being the one "on stage" as well as watching others in this role. It's important to recognize and keep hold of the playfulness of this technique. Done in too somber or heavy-handed a way, the technique of Interactive Modeling will quickly lose its appeal and effectiveness.

To learn more about Interactive Modeling, see *Interactive Modeling: A Powerful Technique for Teaching Children* by Margaret Berry Wilson (Center for Responsive Schools, 2012).

The Teacher as Constant Modeler

When it comes to classroom rules, the adage "Children do as we do, not as we say" couldn't be more true. They learn just as much—if not more—from their spontaneous interactions with us as they do from deliberate lessons. That's why it's so important to pay attention to our own behavior in all interactions with children and adults.

Easier said than done, of course. How many of us have heard ourselves yell at a child, "Do not raise your voice when you talk to me!"? Or speak to a student in a sarcastic or threatening way? Or be dismissive of a parent offering a suggestion for a problem? Just like children, when adults are frustrated or angry, tired or stressed, we often lose control of ourselves and forget or ignore the rules. Knowing that we're doing it may not be enough to make us stop.

The point here is not to be perfect, but to remember that students are watching at all times. With this in mind, try to follow the classroom rules whenever possible, and acknowledge any mistakes you make. A simple "I'm sorry I yelled yesterday. I was feeling angry and I didn't follow our rule about treating others the way we want to be treated" is all that's needed. This shows students that the rules are important—even the teacher tries their best to follow them—and that everyone makes mistakes. It sends the message "We're all learners here, and we don't have to be ashamed of our mistakes."

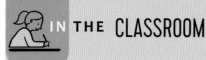

IN THE CLASSROOM

Modeling Procedures and Routines From Day One

Ms. Ghosh, Grade 2 ● On the first day of school, Ms. Ghosh is cautious not to model too much, lest she overwhelm her students. She picks the most essential procedures, always starting with how to respond when she rings the chime for attention. Whole-body listening is another procedure she teaches right away—kneeling or sitting cross-legged, voices off, eyes on the speaker—and she practices with both herself and students as speakers so everyone knows that the expectation is the same, no matter who's talking.

Ms. Meehan, Grade 4 ● Ms. Meehan picks the four or five most important procedures for the first day, focusing on things students need to know how to do right away, such as safely moving their chairs to the meeting circle. She talks with students about the importance of working together, and how these procedures help them do that. She also spends time helping students reflect on why it's important to do things safely and take care of each other.

Mrs. Badge, Grade K ● Kindergartners are so young and so new to school that they need to be taught even the most basic skills. Right at the beginning of the first day, Mrs. Badge models the schoolwide signal for quiet. She also teaches students how to carefully turn and talk with a partner, practicing with a fun and simple topic like what kind of pets they have. She knows she'll need to model everything throughout the year, even things like how to pick up papers from a pile in the middle of the table so that everyone doesn't reach for the top piece and tear it. It's all part of being in kindergarten!

Procedures to Teach at the Beginning of the School Year

While it's best not to overload students on the first day, there are some procedures they need to know right away. These might include some of the following:

- Responding to a signal for quiet
- Moving chairs carefully
- Listening to a speaker
- Lining up
- Walking down the hall
- Going through the cafeteria line
- Using the drinking fountain
- Asking to use or borrow materials
- Sharpening a pencil
- Carrying scissors
- Putting things away in a cubby or storage area

Signals for Quiet

Of the procedures you might teach on the first day, establishing signals for quiet is at the top of the list because of how critical it is to a functioning classroom. Students need to know that you have an effective and calm way to get their attention. This is not something that needs to be discussed and should never be negotiated. You might say, "There'll be lots of times when I or someone else in the classroom needs to get your attention. Here are the signals we'll use for that."

The signals will vary depending on the age of the students, the location (indoors, outdoors, at the meeting area, etc.), and your teaching style. Some common examples include:

- **A visual signal, such as the raising of a hand.** This is used in whole-group meetings or other situations in which everyone can easily see the teacher or whomever needs the group's attention. The person who needs everyone's attention raises a hand. Children who see this may raise their hands as well to help spread the signal. Everyone in the group responds by becoming quiet and turning to the person who wants to speak. This person waits until everyone is paying full attention before beginning.

- **An auditory signal, such as a handclap or the ringing of a chime.** An auditory signal is most often used when children are spread out in the classroom. When the signal is given, everyone ends their conversation and turns to you (or whomever gave the signal). The goal is to teach students to finish their thought and come to a good stopping place, taking a few seconds to do so, before turning their attention back to you. However, younger students may need to start out by learning to "freeze" at the signal, gradually working their way up to finishing their thought over the course of the year.

- **A louder auditory signal for outdoor use, such as blowing a whistle or shouting "Circle up!"** Both of these are effective for getting students' attention when outdoors. In either case, the signal means students should gather around the teacher for further instructions.

In establishing these signals, it's important to be clear about exactly how and why they'll be used. For example, if the goal is to get everyone's quiet attention, is it okay if students raise their hands when they see your hand go up, but then continue to talk with a friend? Is it okay to freeze when the chime rings but not look at the person speaking? Is it okay to continue doodling as long as they're looking at the person speaking? If not, why? Children need clarity about these expectations and the reasons behind them. The more consistent, clear, and firm you are, the more useful the signals will be.

Interactive Modeling:
Responding to an Auditory Signal

1 The teacher says what he will model and why. "I'll often need to get your attention during the day. The chime will help me do that."

2 The teacher models the behavior. The teacher asks for a volunteer to ring the chime. "Ronnie is going to ring the chime, and I'm going to respond. Notice what I do." The teacher begins talking, and Ronnie rings the chime. The teacher takes a moment to finish his thought and then quietly turns his attention to Ronnie.

3 The teacher asks students what they noticed. Students respond, "You finished what you were saying." "You turned your body and looked at Ronnie." "You kept your hands still when you were being quiet."

4 The teacher invites one or more students to model the behavior. Several students volunteer. "This time, Trang and Juan will model having a conversation, and Olivia will ring the chime." The class watches as the students model the behavior.

5 The teacher again asks what students noticed. Students say what they saw and heard. "Trang finished telling Juan about her aunt's visit, but then she stopped." "Juan looked up when he noticed the chime, but then he kept listening to Trang until she was done." "Juan nodded and smiled, but he didn't add anything else." "What did he do?" asks the teacher. The student replies, "He stayed quiet."

6 The whole class practices the behavior. "Now, let's all practice," the teacher says. "Partner up with one of your tablemates and talk for a minute about what you did this past weekend, and then I'll ring the chime."

7 The teacher provides feedback. "I saw people finish their thoughts and respectfully listen to each other, then turn their attention to me. We'll have lots of opportunities to keep practicing each day!"

Expectations for Group Discussions

Other important skills for students to build early on are those related to classroom discussions. If students are going to have group conversations of any substance, they'll need to learn guidelines for doing so in a calm, respectful, and orderly way. Many teachers introduce what they call "meeting guidelines" or "conversation guidelines" during the first week of school. These meeting guidelines consist of four or five statements that name positive behavior expectations such as "Take turns," "Raise your hand if you want to speak," and "Show respect for each other's ideas." You can generate these guidelines alone or with students' input.

> If students are going to have group conversations of any substance, they'll need to learn guidelines for doing so in a calm, respectful, and orderly way.

If you decide to create the guidelines yourself, remember to write them as positive statements, naming your expectations for children's positive behavior. When you present them to the children, link them to a purpose. For example: "In our classroom, there will be many times when we're having large group conversations. It's important that everyone participates in these conversations and that we all feel our ideas are heard. The following guidelines will help ensure that everyone can take part."

If you decide to work with your students to construct the guidelines, be sure to set clear parameters for the task. Let them know that their job is to create guidelines that will help everyone participate in discussions. Be explicit about what is nonnegotiable and, if there are essential guidelines that you feel are missing, be sure to add them.

For example: "I know that if I'm talking and people are moving their bodies a lot or waving their hands to get called on, I get distracted. How about adding, 'Keep your body still when someone is talking' and 'Wait until the person is finished talking before raising your hand'?" If students frame a guideline in the negative, such as "Don't talk when someone is speaking," ask them to reframe it in the positive: "So if we're not going to talk while others are speaking, what should we be doing?"

Once the list seems complete, post the guidelines in the group meeting area and refer students to these guidelines during group conversations, especially during the early weeks of school: "Our guideline says that we should listen when someone is talking" or "Remember, we said we'd raise our hands if we want to say something during a meeting." And remember to reinforce progress: "During our conversation, I noticed that we remembered to raise our hands after a speaker had finished. That's following our meeting guidelines!"

Post the guidelines in the group meeting area and refer students to these guidelines during group conversations.

Creating a Safe and Predictable Learning Environment

1 Organize classroom furniture, supplies, and decor in a way that welcomes students and makes them feel comfortable and safe in the space.

2 Use positive teacher language that helps students envision success, recognize what they're doing well, remember classroom procedures and routines, and get back on task when they lose control.

3 Teach and model expected behaviors using Interactive Modeling, including signals for quiet, group discussion guidelines, and other essential social and academic skills.

Investing Students in the Rules

Investing
Students in the Rules

O nce you have laid the foundation for a healthy and productive learning environment, the work of building the classroom community can proceed in earnest. An essential part of this work is establishing the rules.

Although some students (and adults!) may have negative associations with the idea of rules, having clear, reasonable guidelines for behavior helps students feel safe and participate fully. Rules in the classroom:

- Create a sense of order and predictability

- Create a climate of respect and healthy interactions

- Create an environment in which children feel safe enough to take risks

- Serve as guidelines for behavior to help children learn self-control

- Help children develop social awareness and responsibility

- Balance the needs of the group with the needs of individuals

It's essential to take the time to talk with children about their hopes and dreams to help them set personal learning goals for the year. Whether students want to spend lots of time drawing, learn their multiplication tables, or make new friends this school year, the rules can help them achieve those goals. Once students understand the ways in which the rules support their hopes and dreams, they'll be more likely to view rules as something positive.

Beginning with Hopes and Dreams

For students, thinking about goals can have a profound impact. Inherent in the question "What do you hope to do in school this year?" are the messages that what students care about matters at school, that their hopes and dreams are taken seriously, and that they have a say in what they'll learn.

Students do need guidance in creating goals that are realistic, learning-oriented, and achievable in school. Inevitably, some children will name goals that are not realistic to achieve this year ("Become a doctor") or are not directly related to the work of school ("Make the baseball team"). However, these sorts of goals can still be relevant if you connect them to things students can do in class. The student who wants to become a doctor might set a goal to study hard in science this year, and the student who wants to make the baseball team might choose to focus on practicing teamwork when working with their classmates.

Here are essential ways to ensure that children name goals that are meaningful and achievable in school:

- **Set the context by talking about the work that goes on in classrooms.** Before asking younger students what they hope to accomplish, you might offer a tour of the classroom and talk about some of the things you'll be doing in school this coming year. In the upper elementary grades, ask students to think back on the previous year and name one accomplishment they felt proud of and one thing that was difficult for them. Looking at projects completed by your class in the previous year can help students picture what they themselves will be working on. You might also allow students to start trying out materials like magnetic letters or math manipulatives, and then talk about what they hope to be able to do with those materials by the end of the school year.

- **Express your own hopes and dreams for the school year.** Many teachers think about their own hopes for their students in the coming year and set a goal before asking students to express theirs. For example, a third grade teacher might say: "This year, I hope our classroom will be a safe and caring place to learn and that everyone will do their best work." A fifth grade teacher might say: "This year, I hope that everyone will discover some new books they love to read." Statements such as these set the tone and establish clear expectations about the kind of goals that students will be naming. Just as you can use envisioning language to help students see positive outcomes (see page 21), you can use it to help frame your own goals for the year.

- **Use qualifiers when asking students to name their goals.** Instead of asking "What do you hope to do this year?" ask your students, "What do you hope to learn in our classroom this year?" or "What are some social or academic skills you hope to work on this year in school?" Limiting the question to the arenas of academic and social-emotional skills that are relevant to school helps make sure students name goals that will be attainable.

Hopes and Dreams

Mrs. Badge, Grade K ● Before school starts, Mrs. Badge sends a letter to families to help them start thinking about hopes and dreams. She includes sentence starters for children to answer and parents to record, such as "In kindergarten, I hope I learn . . ." and "In kindergarten, I hope my teacher reads books about . . ." These questions help children better understand what school is all about so that they'll be ready to talk about hopes and dreams once they get there. In her letter, Mrs. Badge also includes a section for parents to fill in with their own hopes and dreams for their child.

Mr. Hunter, Grade 5 ● On the first day of school, Mr. Hunter starts out by giving students a math problem to solve, the answer to which will help them find their assigned seat. Once they get to their seat, they find a survey that asks about their interests, what they enjoyed in the previous school year, what they found most challenging, and what they want to work on. Mr. Hunter spends time with his students discussing why it's important to set goals, and after going through the process of determining hopes and dreams, he has each student set one academic goal and one social or personal goal.

Ms. Meehan, Grade 4 ● Ms. Meehan starts the conversation about hopes and dreams by having students write letters to her about themselves in the first week of school: what subjects they enjoy, where they need practice, what they like doing outside of school, and any other information they think she should know about them. She also asks them to think back on the things they can do now, as new fourth graders, that they couldn't do when they started third grade, and notes how much they will grow this year as well.

Ms. Ghosh, Grade 2 ● Ms. Ghosh often gets the conversation going with read-alouds, using books like *Me . . . Jane* by Patrick McDonnell and *Dex: The Heart of a Hero* by Caralyn Buehner, illustrated by Mark Buehner. These books focus on young characters taking steps in the present to reach big goals for their future. She also emphasizes the importance of keeping discussion lengths appropriate for students' developmental stage, breaking the hopes and dreams conversation into 15- to 20-minute sections for second graders. She might start with a read-aloud and book discussion one day, brainstorm a list of hopes and dreams the next, and so forth, spreading the process over a week so that students are able to stay focused on the task at hand.

Mr. Wade, Grade 3 ● The first week of school is usually a short week, and Mr. Wade spends it observing and getting to know his students. These observations help him prepare to guide discussions about hopes and dreams the following week. He also has his students read books to start thinking about hopes and dreams, such as *The Dot* by Peter H. Reynolds, *Corduroy* by Don Freeman, and *Thank You, Mr. Falker* by Patricia Polacco. Once he's ready to start the conversation, he asks, "Why do we come to school?" Students give all kinds of answers, some funny ("It's the law!" "My parents need a break!") and some serious ("I want to be a better reader." "I want to make friends"). Then he asks, "Out of all the things we listed, what do you want most from third grade?" This question, along with a list of things the class will do and learn about over the course of the year, helps children focus in on their own hopes and dreams.

Once students have determined their hopes and dreams, it's time to share them with the class. This can be done by having each student share their own goal in a whole-class discussion, having students share with a partner and then tell the class about their partner's goal, or having students work independently to draw or write about their goal. Then, post students' hopes and dreams where the whole class can see them, talk about them, and refer back to them as the year progresses. No matter how students share their hopes and dreams, doing so helps children develop an awareness of and appreciation for what's important to each of their classmates.

Displaying hopes and dreams offers a great opportunity to get creative, allow students to express themselves, and develop a shared sense of identity in the classroom. Different ideas for displaying hopes and dreams include the following:

- Have children draw, paint, or make a collage to illustrate their most important hope for the year, and record their words on the picture. Mr. Wade types each of his third graders' hopes and dreams on a label to place on their illustration so they can focus on the activity without being distracted if they are not yet comfortable with writing.

- Display students' work all together as a "Hopes and Dreams" bulletin board.

- Post individual goals around the room as Ms. Ghosh does, which allows her second graders to see goals everywhere they look (and brightens up beginning-of-year bare classroom walls).

- Provide a theme for students' illustrations to follow as Ms. Meehan does, such as clouds to represent dreams, squares of a quilt to represent everyone working together, or superhero emblems students create for themselves. Or, open it up to students' ideas and have them vote on their favorite. "One student suggested we create a house and all our goals will be the windows," Ms. Meehan says. "Another student said that we should create a giant book and our goals will be the words on the pages. Letting them have input really helped them have ownership of the project!"

- Take a picture of each student and post it next to that student's goal like Mrs. Badge does. This lets her kindergartners see themselves and think about their hopes and dreams even if they're not yet able to independently read their names or the hopes and dreams that are posted on the wall.

- Let students walk around and see everyone's hopes and dreams after they've been posted. Ask what they notice about each other's work. Treat this time like a celebration to get students excited about achieving their hopes and dreams this year!

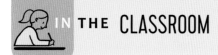

IN THE CLASSROOM

Connecting With Families

Mr. Wade, Grade 3 • After the first week of school has gone by, Mr. Wade likes to call each child's family to check in and see how things have been going. But what parents aren't expecting is that he asks to speak to their child first! He asks what the student liked about their first week of school and what they're looking forward to in third grade. Only then does he talk to parents, and frequently, they comment on how much they saw their child beaming because of the attention he gave them on the phone. This starts the parent-teacher relationship off on a positive note, which helps parents open up and give more meaningful responses when he asks how their child's first week went: How has the child reacted to school so far? Have they been tired, upset, excited? Is there anything else they'd like him to know?

*About the Term "Parent"

Many children are being raised by grandparents, siblings, aunts and uncles, foster families, and other caregivers. All of these individuals are to be honored for devoting their time, attention, and love to raising children. In this book, for ease of reading, the term "parent" is used to represent all the caregivers involved in a child's life.

You may also choose to invite parents* into the process of articulating hopes for the year. Inviting parents to express their own hopes for their child is a good way to build rapport with them and help them start to develop a sense of trust in you as their child's teacher. Here are a few possible ways to do this:

- At the first parent-teacher conference (preferably before the first day of school), share your hope for the year. Then, ask parents to share theirs: "What's your most important hope for your child in school this year?" or "What do you think is most important for your child to learn in school this year?" Sending this question to parents ahead of time will give them time to think about it before the conference.

- Before school starts or early in the year, send a letter to parents explaining the goal-setting process and inviting them to write back with their goals for their child this year. Some teachers ask parents specifically to share an academic goal and a social goal. Others leave the question more open-ended. You could also choose to gather more general information from parents about their child's strengths, challenges, likes, and dislikes, and guide them in setting a goal for their child in person at the first parent-teacher conference.

- In preparation for the first open house, create a display showing all of the students' goals for the year. Students can write a personal letter to their parents asking them to share their most important hopes for the child's school year.

Sample Letter to Parents About Hopes and Dreams

Dear Parents:

Our back-to-school night will be held on Wednesday, August 20, from 6:00 to 8:00 p.m. I'm excited to meet you and give you the chance to start exploring our classroom! This event will let us start building a positive relationship with each other so that we can all better support your child's learning.

At this first meeting, I will be asking you to share your hopes and dreams for your child in school this year. Please think about an academic goal and a social goal for us to focus on together. I will be paying careful attention to these goals and keeping you informed of your child's progress throughout the year. At our conference, I will also share my own social and academic goals for the class this year.

In the first weeks of school, everyone in the class will think about what they most want to learn and do in school this year. All the children will share their hopes and dreams with the class. Then the class will create classroom rules that will support all class members in achieving their goals.

In the middle of the year, we will evaluate your child's growth and decide whether to continue with the goals you and your child chose, or to choose new goals. I look forward to meeting with you and working together to make this a safe, challenging, and joyful year for your child!

Sincerely,

Connecting Goals to Rules

Allowing students to take part in the rule-creation process increases their sense of ownership of the rules and their desire to follow them. The collaborative approach to rule-making starts with discussing hopes, dreams, and goals as outlined on pages 43–47. The next step is to ask, "If these are our hopes and dreams, what rules will we need to help us make them come true?" Thinking through this question helps students make the important connection between their personal hopes for the year and the classroom rules. It also helps them to see that everyone's goals are important and that the rules are there to help everyone succeed. If students do not understand these points, the rules will hold little meaning.

Co-creating the Rules With Students

There are various ways to start generating ideas for rules. Some teachers begin with a whole-group discussion: "If Niloufer wants to learn Spanish, what rules will we need to help her reach this goal? What rules will we need to help Markus reach his goal of making new friends?" Students who are a little older might instead do a writing exercise to brainstorm possible rules to help them reach their goals. Or, they might discuss ideas with a partner, then share those ideas with the larger group.

As the discussion progresses, write down the ideas students generate on a whiteboard or chart paper. For any rules that are expressed in the negative, ask the student to restate their idea as a positive. For instance, if a student suggests, "Don't mess up other people's work," ask what people should do instead. "Respect each other's work," the student might say. By framing the rules in the positive, the emphasis shifts from rules that foster compliance to rules that foster self-control and a sense of responsibility to the group. They are constant reminders of what everyone in the classroom, including the teachers, are striving to become. They represent the community's ideals.

IN THE CLASSROOM

Co-creating the Rules

Mr. Wade, Grade 3 • First, Mr. Wade asks students, "In order for your hopes and dreams to become true, what do you need from your classmates and me?" He then gives each table cluster a stack of sticky notes and has them write down as many rules as they can think of. The class usually comes up with over 100 rules! Mr. Wade collects all the ideas and says, "Wow! That's a lot of rules. I need to take these home and study them." This lets students know that he takes this work seriously and that they're always on his mind. The next day, he says, "I'm overwhelmed by all these rules. Can we group them all under these four categories?" Students then have good conversations about which category each rule fits in.

Mr. Hunter, Grade 5 • Mr. Hunter uses structured collaborative activities to ensure that the rule-creation process is active and that everyone in class is involved. After the class has brainstormed a long list of rules, he not only asks them to group rules that are related but also asks why those rules go to-gether. This gets students thinking critically about the rules and what they really mean.

Ms. Meehan, Grade 4 • In Ms. Meehan's class, students get into small groups of four or five to sort the rules into different categories that they come up with. Each group makes a poster of their catego-ries and displays it for the rest of the class to see. The next day, the class comes back together as a whole group and consolidates the categories the small groups created into three or four, which they then turn into rules together. When they have their full list, they write it up, post it, and sign it.

Ms. Ghosh, Grade 2 • After the class has brainstormed a list of rules, Ms. Ghosh works with students to group similar items, circling them in the same color. She then groups the color-coded ideas into three to five lists. The next day, students help to come up with titles for each of these lists, and those titles become the rules. Students vote with thumbs up, down, or sideways to indicate that they approve, disapprove, or want to suggest a wording change.

Mrs. Badge, Grade K • With her kindergartners, Mrs. Badge uses the word "promises" instead of "rules" to talk about guidelines that help everyone achieve their hopes and dreams. The children start by brainstorming promises: "I promise I'll be nice to my friend," "I promise to put my coat away." Mrs. Badge then helps them group these promises, steering the children to identify the three overall promises of being kind, taking care of things, and listening (later, she adds "I promise to take care of my own learning" once children are better able to understand what that means). She writes the promises and posts them near the Morning Meeting spot, and she and the students recite them each day.

After generating this long list of ideas, the next step is to go through the list with students and have them group similar ideas in order to narrow the rules down to a few general, easy-to-remember statements. A short list of broad rules fosters ethical thinking and the practice of self-control by giving children the opportunity to apply general behavior expectations to various situations. You might begin the consolidation process by saying, "This is a great list of rules, but there are so many of them. I know that I won't be able to remember all these rules. I wonder if we can put some of them together so that we only have a few rules to remember."

To begin, you might choose to give students a set of around four general categories under which to group their ideas. These categories typically have to do with:

- Taking care of ourselves
- Taking care of others
- Taking care of our classroom and materials
- Taking care to do our best work

A short list of broad rules fosters ethical thinking and the practice of self-control.

With students who are a little older, you might ask for input to determine what the sorting categories will be. In all likelihood, the categories students come up with will be very similar to the ones stated above: care for ourselves, care for others, care for materials, and care for our work. But the process of sorting and synthesizing lets students gain a depth of understanding—of the meaning of the rules and of each other—that may not otherwise be possible.

When all the rules have been sorted into categories, the class might want to adjust the wording of the categories. It is always illuminating to hear which words students choose to use—their words are a clue to what they really understand the rules to mean. And because their words are a way for students to communicate nuances of understanding to each other, it's appropriate to let students spend some time crafting the wording together. That said, keep in mind that the exact wording of the final rules is less important than the process of getting to them. Try not to let the class, especially if it's a group of passionate debaters, get too hung up on the details of the wording.

Here are examples of the final list of rules—global, positive, and few in number—from classrooms at two different grade levels.

Second grade classroom	Fourth grade classroom
Take care of yourself and keep everybody safe.	Be in control of yourself.
Help and respect other people.	Be helpful and respectful of others.
Be gentle and take care of all the things in our school.	Treat people the way you want to be treated.
Take care of your own learning.	Be a thinking worker.

The Golden Rule and Other Tricky Topics

Often, children come up with some version of the Golden Rule—"Treat others as you'd like to be treated"—as one of their classroom rules. While this is an accepted tenet in many traditions, it can be confusing for children, who may take this saying literally. While a literal understanding works in some situations ("If I want people to share the markers with me, I have to share the markers with them"), it doesn't work in others ("If I don't mind when people tease me about my clothes, then it's okay for me to tease others about their clothes").

For this reason, if your students come up with the Golden Rule, make it a point to talk with them about what it really means. Help students understand that the rule is about the broad idea of treating others with respect and care, just as you'd like to be treated with respect and care. Part of living by the rule is learning what respect and care look, sound, and feel like to the other person rather than using oneself as the standard. With this shared understanding, children will be more able to make sense of the Golden Rule and use it in their everyday school life.

Other rules, such as "Try your best" or "Have fun" may sound good on the surface, but can be tough to implement. Trying one's best is very subjective—for a student experiencing extreme trauma, learning disabilities, or other challenges, trying their best may look very different than it would for a student without those struggles. One student's maximum effort might look like another's minimum, and feeling that they're not measuring up can discourage students who are already struggling.

Similarly, "fun" will look different in different children. One student might find it fun to sit at their desk and get lost in thought as they write a story, while another student might find it more fun to run and jump around on the playground. Students may ask, "If I'm not having fun in math, does that mean I don't have to do it?" Providing lessons that are fun for students—that is, lessons that allow for meaningful engagement and challenge—is a good goal for teachers, but having fun isn't something that can be mandated. If students propose these sorts of rules, help them navigate toward more achievable, universal ones.

Using Existing Rules

There are times when you might need to present a set of rules to the class rather than creating the rules with students—for example, due to school or district requirements. When making those rules, educators may choose to work together using the steps described on pages 50–53 for collaborative rule-making (considering goals, writing a long list of specific rules, restating them in the positive, and grouping them into categories). Teachers can also begin with rules they've used in years past and adapt them for the needs of this year's students. If there are schoolwide rules in place, think about how to adapt them to meet your classroom goals and needs. Ideally, teachers and administrators should think about creating rules that are global, few in number, and positively stated.

For example, this set of rules is simple and kid-friendly:

- Be safe and kind.
- Take care of yourself.
- Take care of our room.

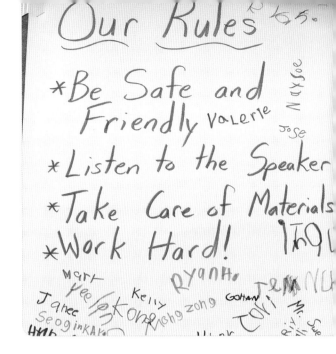

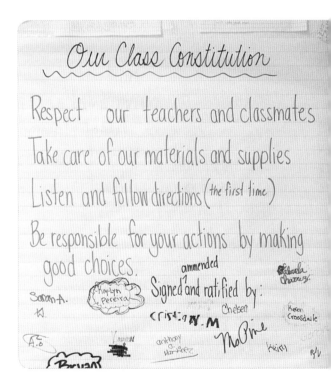

IN THE CLASSROOM

Living by the Rules

Ms. Meehan, Grade 4 ● Once the rules have been established and discussed with students, Ms. Meehan frequently mentions the rules and reminds students why the class does things the way it does. "Remember the way we learned to carry the scissors?" she might ask. "Which rule connects to why we learned to do it that way?"

Ms. Ghosh, Grade 2 ● Ms. Ghosh connects the rules with academics whenever she can. For example, the first social studies unit she teaches in the fall is on civics and citizenship, which provides ample opportunities to discuss how rules apply in a larger context.

Mr. Hunter, Grade 5 ● When creating the rules, Mr. Hunter tells his students that he likes to think about the rules as a set of understandings we live by, like the Constitution. After the class has finalized the list of rules, he turns those rules into their classroom constitution, documenting them on parchment complete with "We the People" written at the top. Everyone in the class signs the classroom constitution, and they hold a ceremony to post it. Mr. Hunter wants students to feel the importance of the work they've done, and to understand that this is their classroom and what they think matters.

Post the list of rules in a visible spot in the classroom and refer to them often in the early days of the school year. When teaching and modeling procedures as outlined in the previous chapter, reference the rules in step one of Interactive Modeling when you explain why students will be learning a particular procedure: "Today, I'll show you how to use the markers in a way that helps us follow our rule to take care of our room." "We're going to learn how to listen to someone who's talking so that we can follow our rule to be kind." Note that in both of these examples, the teacher refers to "our rules" to help students build a sense of ownership of those rules.

It's also important to build ownership of the rules by connecting them to students' hopes, dreams, and goals for the year. When initiating the discussion about hopes and dreams, make sure to wait long enough that children feel safe in the classroom and positive enough about school to engage in a meaningful discussion about their goals. And you might not go through every step in the process described on pages 43–47. Instead, choose those steps you think the children in your classroom can engage in most productively.

After students have chosen their goal for the year, go through the class rules with them again and have them think about how one or more of the rules connects with their goal. To give an example, you might say, "My goal for this year is for our class to be a welcoming place where everyone can learn. That connects to our rule to be safe and kind, because if people are kind to each other, that will help everyone feel welcome." Having students consider these connections helps them understand that the rules exist to help them—and everyone else in class—achieve their goals. Once they have this understanding, the rules become more valuable and meaningful to students.

Some teachers may choose a hybrid approach to rule-making where they create the rules themselves, but do so with input from students. For example, you might start out with a discussion about hopes, dreams, and goals and then use the information you learn from students to create the rules. Or, you might explicitly ask students what kinds of rules might help them meet their goals (see pages 50–53), and then narrow down the final list yourself. Alternately, you could state the rules on day one but choose a time later in the year to engage in a modified version of the collaborative process to amend the initial rules.

It's important to build ownership of the rules by connecting them to students' hopes, dreams, and goals for the year.

Celebrating and Sharing the Rules

No matter how the rules are created, once students have discussed how those rules can help them meet their goals, it's fitting for the class to celebrate these rules and share them with students' families. Here are a few ideas you might use:

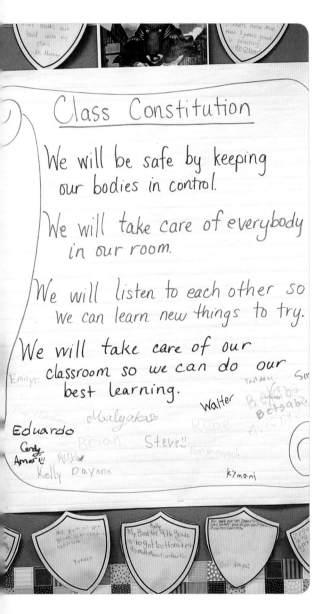

- **Send a letter home to parents.** In the letter, celebrate the classroom rules and ask for parents' support. (See the sample letter at right.)

- **Have students make a beautiful display of the rules.** Perhaps they can write the final rules on a large poster board and surround it with illustrations. In some classes, all students sign the poster to show that they agree to try to live by the rules. Display the poster in a prominent place in the room.

- **Invite families to the classroom for a rule-signing celebration.** Have a poster of the rules ready for students to sign ceremoniously in the presence of their families. If students helped create the rules, they can prepare a brief presentation for parents on how these rules came to be.

Sample Letter to Parents About Classroom Rules

Dear Parents,

We have been talking a lot during these early weeks of school about our goals for this school year. Students have worked hard to discover topics they'll learn, reflect on what they are able to do now that they couldn't last year, and build excitement for what is to come this year.

Some students have set specific goals to develop an academic or social skill, and others have hopes that they will grow as learners and contributing community members. All of our hopes and dreams are important. To create a climate where each of us can achieve our goals, we created these rules to follow.

[List the classroom rules.]

You can help us at home. Please keep this list in a prominent place and review the rules often with your child. We are all working together to create a safe and caring community of learners. I appreciate your support. Please feel free to call me if you have questions about these rules or my approach to classroom discipline.

Sincerely,

Helping Students Follow the Rules

Establishing classroom rules is a good starting point for a year of positive behavior. But just because children can articulate the rules doesn't mean they will always follow them. Controlling impulses, expressing feelings in a constructive way, and momentarily putting personal needs aside for the good of the group are complex, demanding skills—skills that even adults struggle with. Many of us have had the experience of interrupting someone even though we know it's rude or raising our voice even though we know we're acting out of anger.

If living by accepted codes of behavior and rules is challenging for adults, it can be downright hard for children. Students in elementary school are just beginning to learn self-control, communication skills, perspective taking, and the myriad other skills needed to live and learn peacefully with others. To be successful, they need lots of encouragement, support, and practice, practice, practice—without judgment or criticism. The goals of practicing positive behavior with students are to:

- Further students' understanding of behavior expectations

- Help students understand how general expectations (like being respectful) translate into concrete actions

- Establish clear and specific behavior expectations for various settings (such as in reading groups, in the meeting area, at recess, or when there's a guest teacher)

- Encourage ethical thinking and internalization of classroom rules

- Acknowledge that living by classroom rules can be hard, and support children in correcting and learning from their mistakes

Practicing positive behavior is done continuously throughout the year, as part of planned lessons and in the moment, as needed. There are a number of specific strategies teachers can use to help students apply the rules to day-to-day classroom life. These may include:

- Teacher language that reinforces, reminds, and redirects students as they apply the rules to their daily lives (see pages 22–26)

- Structured discussion to help children apply general guidelines to specific situations (see pages 62–63)

- Interactive Modeling to teach and rehearse appropriate behaviors in situations where there is one specific way to do something (see pages 28–31)

- Role-plays to help students prepare for situations where there is more than one way to do something (see pages 65–67)

IN THE CLASSROOM

Connecting to the Rules

Mr. Hunter, Grade 5 • If Mr. Hunter hasn't made three to five connections to the rules each day, he feels like he hasn't done his job: to keep the classroom constitution living and show how it connects to everything. These connections can be private to reinforce or redirect an individual student's behavior, or they can be public to reinforce when the whole class has been living the classroom constitution. Mr. Hunter does his best to be open with students about his own mistakes in order to build an atmosphere of safety and trust, and to show students that we all make mistakes and we can all take responsibility for them.

> To be successful, students need lots of encouragement, support, and practice, practice, practice— without judgment or criticism.

Structured Discussion

"Our rules say we will respect each other. What will that look like and sound like when we're in reading groups today?" If children are to learn to think for themselves and make ethical decisions about their behavior, we need to help them translate the rules into specific actions and words that constitute positive behavior.

A powerful way to do this is through discussion of how the rules apply in a number of different situations. These discussions don't need to be long or weighty. In fact, it's best if they are brief and immediate, closely linked in time to the activity or situation. For example, in preparing children for recess, you might say, "Our rules say that we will take care of each other and keep people safe. What's one thing you'll do to keep your classmates safe when you're on the playground today?" The students might respond, "Tag gently," "Help someone if they fall down," or "Let everyone play."

Discussions can also happen after an event to help students reflect on their behavior. For example, after recess, you might ask: "What was the hardest rule to follow during recess today? What could we do better next time?" Frequent short discussions like these help children make important connections between behavior expectations and their actions.

In both of these examples, open-ended questions help get the discussion started. Open-ended questions are those for which there is no one right or wrong answer. Instead, any reasoned and relevant answer is correct. Open-ended questions can spark useful discussions because they challenge students to think deeply about a situation, draw on prior knowledge, and listen carefully to one another's ideas.

Here are some tips for asking effective open-ended questions:

- **Be clear about what you're asking for.** A question such as "How did we do during recess?" might be too general for most children to respond to easily. Instead, clarify what it is about recess you are asking them to reflect on. For example: "What were some ways you followed our rule to take care of each other during recess?"

- **Be genuinely curious and avoid pseudo open-ended questions.** If you ask a question with an idea in mind about how children should answer, they'll know that you're not really interested in hearing their responses. Instead, cultivate genuine curiosity about children's thinking—and only open these discussions when you are interested in hearing children's thoughts.

The timing and format of structured discussions will vary depending on children's ages and their ability to think reflectively about their behavior. With young children or those who have little experience reflecting on behavior, start small and structure the discussions carefully. For example, you might focus on one question, using language that relates to children's daily lives. When wiggliness starts to take over, it's time to stop the discussion. With older children, who might have a more sophisticated ability to reflect on behavior and feelings, these discussions can be more wide-ranging.

At any age, a useful strategy for guiding the discussion is the T-chart, which provides a concrete structure to help children apply abstract rules to specific situations. You might ask, "What would our rule to take care of our classroom environment look like during choice time? What would it sound like?" As children give their responses, fill in the appropriate columns on the chart, which then gets posted for ongoing reference.

Revisiting the Rules at Midyear

Ms. Ghosh, Grade 2 ● Discussion of the rules and how to follow them shouldn't end in September. Ms. Ghosh suggests revisiting the topic of hopes and dreams in January, right after winter break, often connecting them to the idea of New Year's resolutions. She asks students to set new goals if they've reached the ones they set at the beginning of the school year, and write them on a sticky note to place over their original goals to see their progress. She also holds more active discussions about the rules and models any procedures and routines that have gotten rusty while students were on vacation over the previous few weeks.

Ms. Meehan, Grade 4 ● Ms. Meehan likes to revisit the rules in January to see if they still fit "midyear fourth graders." She gives students the chance to vote on whether the rules are still useful as is or if they need to be changed. Sometimes, simply rewording a rule makes it fresh again. This process allows students to be reflective about the rules and realign them as needed to meet their current developmental stage.

Mrs. Badge, Grade K ● After winter break, Mrs. Badge's students have a better understanding of what kindergarten is all about than they had at the beginning of the year. This is a good time to look at students' hopes and dreams and talk about any changes or additions children want to make. Mrs. Badge types up these revisions and puts them over the original hopes and dreams so that students can see them both.

Mr. Hunter, Grade 5 ● Mr. Hunter does a midyear check-in with his students about the ways they feel they've been successful in living by the classroom constitution. This reinforcement honors their commitment to the classroom community. Though the class rarely feels the need to update the rules at midyear, Mr. Hunter does talk about how there can be amendments to a constitution if any rules need to be expanded upon or clarified.

When Working With a Partner we...

* Share
* Listen to each other
* Help each other
* Talk to solve problems.
* Speak quietly
* Be polite
* Take turns
* Encourage each other

Role-Playing

Role-playing prepares students for more complex social interactions. Unlike Interactive Modeling, which shows how to follow a procedure that should be performed in one specific way, role-playing is used to demonstrate scenarios that can be handled in many positive ways. For example, role-playing can help students think about how to include someone in an activity, how to be a good sport when they're winning or losing a game, and how to respectfully disagree with a partner's ideas. Role-playing acknowledges the complexity of these situations and gives students practice in making responsible choices.

It's best if situations chosen for role-playing spring from the life of the classroom. For example, you may know from experience that students at certain ages are likely to:

- Have difficulty sharing materials

- Laugh at or show intolerance for another's mistakes

- Become inflamed over accidents, such as someone knocking something over

- Exclude certain students

Choose one issue at a time to role-play. First, reframe the problem in positive terms. For example:

- "Students have difficulty sharing materials" might become "We are going to brainstorm how we can share our supplies."

- "Students laugh at another's mistakes" might be reframed as "We are going to practice being supportive when someone makes a mistake."

- "Students exclude one another at recess" might become "We are going to think of ways to include other people during recess."

IN THE CLASSROOM

Role-Playing

Mr. Hunter, Grade 5

Where children are developmentally informs many of the issues they face in the classroom. There are "fifth grade problems" Mr. Hunter sees all the time, many of which are related to social dynamics. Understanding students' developmental stages helps him anticipate these challenges and proactively do role-playing to help students be ready to handle these issues when they happen.

Mrs. Badge, Grade K

Though the full process of role-playing may be a little complex for kindergartners, asking "What do you do if . . . ?" is a good way to help children start preparing for this process. Mrs. Badge finds that many kindergartners are still learning how to play with others, so she asks a lot of questions to help them learn: "What do you do if someone else has the toy you want?" "What do you do if you don't know who to play with at recess?"

Once you have established the positive goal of the role-play, work collaboratively with students to name and act out possible behaviors. While the goal itself is never negotiable—for example, deciding not to be inclusive is not an option—there can be several routes to achieving that goal. After seeing several possible solutions enacted, students will have an expanded repertoire of behavior choices when faced with the real-life situation.

Following are the steps typically used in a role-play, illustrated with the example of a class learning what to do when they really want to say something during someone else's sharing.

1. **Describe a specific situation, using language that will bring the scene to life for students.** Stop the narration just before the point where a behavior decision—and a possible conflict—will occur. "Imagine that it's sharing time and a classmate—we'll call her Sarah—begins to share about visiting her cousin who's home from college. I just visited my cousin, too. I'm so excited. I want to tell someone about my visit, but I know I need to listen to Sarah."

2. **Name the positive goal, connecting it to classroom rules.** "Our classroom rule says 'Respect each other.' How can I be a respectful listener when I'm eager to say something myself?"

3. **Invite and record children's ideas for solutions, being sure the ideas are framed positively.** After thinking for a minute, students begin calling out ideas: "You need to sit quietly until Sarah's finished, but I bet you'll look really interested!" "When Sarah's done, you could ask her a question." "You could go up to Sarah later and tell her about your visit. Maybe the two of you could talk about it during lunch."

4. **Act out one idea, with the teacher in the lead—or "tricky"—role.** Taking the lead role at this point allows you to control the tone of the role-play. The teacher decides to act out the first idea the class gave. She asks for a volunteer to play Sarah, and then sits with an erect, alert posture and an interested smile while listening to Sarah's sharing. She waits until Sarah has finished, raises her hand, and asks Sarah a follow-up question.

5 Ask students what they noticed, prompting them as needed to notice tone of voice, specific words used, and body language. "What did you notice about my behavior?" the teacher asks the class. The students say she sat up straight, looked Sarah in the eye, and looked excited about what Sarah was saying but didn't try to interrupt.

6 Act out another idea. Choose new actors and, if you think students are ready for it, have a student play the lead role this time.

7 Again, ask children what they noticed.

8 Continue acting out other ideas.

9 Sum up lessons learned. Briefly reiterate the strategies tried and re-inforce how they meet the positive goal you originally stated. "So, here are the ideas we acted out for being a respect-ful listener when we're really eager to talk ourselves: Sit quietly until the person's finished, but look really interested; ask the person a question after they finish; and tell the person you're really interested in the topic later, and talk with them about it at a good time, like during lunch. These are all ways to live out our classroom rule 'Respect each other.'"

10 Follow up. In the days and weeks ahead, remind students of these strategies before they go into potentially tricky situations. "What were some of the strategies we thought of to be respectful listeners during presentations?" Afterwards, let them know that you noticed their use of the strategies. "I saw students' eyes on the speaker and heard students holding their questions and comments until after the speaker was done."

To learn more about role-playing, see *Solving Thorny Behavior Problems: How Teachers and Students Can Work Together* by Caltha Crowe (Center for Responsive Schools, 2009).

Helping Students Get Back in Control of Their Behavior

So now, the rules have been established. Students have connected those rules to their own goals and discussed how the rules will look and sound in a variety of situations. They've learned and practiced the classroom procedures and routines, and they've role-played situations that may arise during the school day. They're as prepared as possible to follow the rules. Yet, sometimes, behavior will still go off course.

One of the essential functions of the teacher is to manage the classroom in a way that lets students know where the boundaries and limits are. Helping students just as behavior begins to go off task lets them get back in control before misbehaviors escalate, and it helps the class as a whole stay focused on learning. Chapter 3 contains more extensive information on responding to misbehavior, but here are some ways to intervene when students are just beginning to stray from the rules.

Use Visual and Verbal Cues

Steve rolls his eyes at a friend while another student is sharing. Marianne starts to fiddle with the puzzles on the shelf behind her during a lesson. Pauline whispers to her neighbor instead of doing her math work. Yaser cuts in line. Before a whisper turns into a conversation or a cut in line turns into a fight, a simple visual or verbal cue can help students refocus and quickly get back on task. Essentially, the cue communicates, "I know that you understand the rules. Now let's see you put them into action."

Here are some common and effective visual and verbal cues:

- Make brief eye contact with the child.

- Say the child's name.

- Nod at the child.

- Give a hand signal, such as a writing gesture or a finger against the lips.

- Use reminding or redirecting language, such as "What do our rules say about sharing materials?" or "Quiet feet, Sean." (See pages 23–26 for more information on reminding and redirecting language.)

Notice that none of these cues require you to stop what you're doing or explain the rule or expectation. These cues also minimize calling attention to the child. The communication is between you and the student involved. You assume that the student knows what to do but just needs a little nudge to do it.

These simple cues are most effective when they're given before behavior has gone far off task. Obviously, if a child doesn't immediately respond to a visual or verbal cue, then it's time to be more directive (see Chapter 3). However, giving children the opportunity to recognize their mistakes and correct themselves in the moment helps them to preserve their dignity and develop self-control.

When using visual cues and gestures, it's important to pay attention to our own body language. If we are feeling angry or frustrated, even simple eye contact might carry a punitive message. Maintaining a calm, neutral expression and demeanor lets students know that we are there to help—not to judge or criticize.

Increase Teacher Proximity

Sometimes all that's needed to reestablish positive behavior is for a teacher to move next to a child. For example, if first grader Maria is kicking the rungs of her chair during a classmate's presentation, her teacher might simply stand next to her, which can be a cue to Maria to have quiet feet. The teacher would continue to stand there for a minute or so to ensure that Maria's feet do indeed stay still.

Don't Overuse Cues and Reminders

All this said, keep in mind that cues and reminders can have a negative effect if they're overused. In classrooms where teachers always give a certain number of reminders before taking further action, students quickly figure out that they don't really have to control themselves right away. If the teacher tells a student to stop poking his neighbor four times before sending him to time-out, or comes over and repeatedly stands next to two students who are whispering to each other but doesn't separate them, students become more focused on keeping track of the reminders than on keeping track of their own behavior. Remember, these cues are intended to help students gain self-control and improve their ability to follow the rules on their own.

Investing Students in the Rules

1 Begin by discussing students' hopes and dreams for the school year and picking one goal to focus on.

2 Connect students' goals to the rules, whether those rules are established by the teacher or created collaboratively with the class.

3 Help students follow the rules through Interactive Modeling, positive teacher language, structured discussion, and role-playing.

4 At the first signs of behavior getting off task, help students get back in control with visual and verbal cues and increased teacher proximity.

Responding to Misbehavior

Responding to Misbehavior

By taking the proactive steps outlined in the first two chapters of this book, you're already doing a lot of the work of discipline. But there will still be times when you need to respond to children's misbehavior. The proactive work can make those responses more effective and reduce the amount of time spent responding to behavior issues, but it won't completely eliminate children's misbehavior. After all, part of school is about learning how to behave appropriately, and making mistakes is part of learning.

In this chapter, you'll learn disciplinary techniques that can be applied to many kinds of common misbehaviors, from whispering during a lesson to misusing classroom materials. These are the sorts of everyday lapses in following the rules that occur occasionally with every child. The focus of this chapter is on individual instances of misbehavior rather than ongoing or more serious behavior issues, which will be covered in Chapters 4 and 5.

Why Do Children Misbehave?

It's not hard to understand why children break the rules sometimes. Just think about all the reasons you might have for breaking a rule. For example, if you're in the 12-items-or-less checkout aisle at the grocery store but you have 15 items in your basket, you might be doing it because:

- You're running late and this was the shortest line.
- You didn't know there was a 12-item limit.
- You don't think it should be a 12-item limit.
- You don't think you'll get caught.
- You like how it feels to get away with it.
- You didn't know how many items you had in your basket.
- You're frustrated that your last meeting went so late and it's "their" fault you have to break the rules now.
- Everyone else has more than 12 items.

Like adults, children will have many moments when impulse wins over reason, desire over logic, feelings over rational thought. They will get curious, they will get carried away, they will forget. As every adult knows, it can take a lifetime to learn how to control one's impulses and regulate one's behavior.

> As every adult knows, it can take a lifetime to learn how to control one's impulses and regulate one's behavior.

Also keep in mind that children are still in the early stages of learning the rules of the world, not just the rules of the classroom. They're constantly trying to figure out what the larger world expects of them, and they do much of this learning by doing. Through their exploring and experimenting, they come to understand what's acceptable and what isn't on the playground, at the dinner table, during sports practice, at an assembly, on the bus.

Responding to Misbehavior

Mr. Wade, Grade 3 A proactive discussion about breaking the rules helps Mr. Wade reassure his students that they can talk openly about making mistakes. He gives an example from his own life (getting a speeding ticket), and then asks students, "Have you ever broken the rules?" The class shares stories, and they talk about them together. For example, one student who secretly stayed up past his bedtime playing video games fell asleep and got caught in front of the television in the morning. "How did you feel when that happened?" Mr. Wade asked the student. He always makes the point that we all break rules, sometimes on purpose and sometimes by accident. This lays the foundation for a conversation about ways he'll respond to misbehavior in the classroom.

Mrs. Badge, Grade K • Empathy is essential when responding to mistakes and misbehavior. Mrs. Badge keeps her responses simple and kind when a student misbehaves: "Oh, it's a bummer that that happened. Here's how we fix it." Her school has kid-sized cleaning supplies to let children help clean up simple messes they've made, and she guides children in practicing skills that will help them follow the rules.

Mr. Hunter, Grade 5 • When responding to misbehavior, Mr. Hunter always tries to connect his reminders and redirections back to students' goals so that they know that he's doing it for them, not for himself. He keeps feedback private, looks for the positive in students, and strives to build their empathy. For example, with a student who's been blurting out comments during class discussions, he might say, "I noticed you're really engaged and eager to share. When you blurt something out, that may inhibit someone else who's eager to share. It's important to make sure everyone who wants to can share. That connects to our rule 'Consider our impact.'"

Experimenting with rules and testing limits is a normal part of children's development. It's how they construct their understanding of social expectations. And while some children are much more persistent in their testing than others, almost every child has some need to experiment with behavior. Child psychologist Robert MacKenzie describes children's misbehavior as research, testing the limits in order to find out how the adults in their lives will respond. With their misbehavior, these young researchers are asking, "What's OK? What's not OK? Who's in control? How far can I go? And what happens when I go too far?" (MacKenzie 1997, 32–34).

In the process of doing this testing and experimenting, students will make lots of mistakes. Just as with learning an academic subject such as math or reading or science, students need regular practice to solidify their learning about positive behavior expectations. Teachers can use students' mistakes as opportunities to teach self-control and responsibility.

To do this, it's important to maintain empathy. Having empathy doesn't mean letting go of accountability. Hold children accountable, but with understanding and curiosity for why they might be misbehaving—and faith that they can choose a better way to behave.

Goals in Responding to Misbehavior

The number one priority in responding to misbehavior is to stop the negative behavior and reestablish positive behavior as quickly and simply as possible so that the child can return to learning and the teacher can focus on teaching. Doing this is essential to maintaining a safe and orderly classroom.

It's also important to give children opportunities to learn from their mistakes. Rather than simply telling children what to do, we need to help them develop their own understanding of why it's not safe to run in the halls, why it's distracting to a speaker when classmates are poking each another, and why it's hurtful to laugh at someone. It is through making mistakes; experiencing relevant, nonpunitive consequences; and, when appropriate, processing the mistakes with a caring adult that students eventually internalize the rules and learn to take responsibility for their actions.

To respond effectively to children's misbehavior, it is important to begin with the assumption of children's good intentions and not make snap judgments when incidents occur. When we see Lily ripping up Arnold's writing assignment, we don't know what Arnold wrote about Lily on that paper. When we see Juan jab Mike, we don't know what Mike might have done to provoke it. And when Penelope pounds her desk in frustration during writing time, we have no idea what might have happened to prompt such anger before Penelope came to school that morning.

Rather than making quick, negative judgments—Lily is up to her antics again, Juan is so aggressive, Penelope is always trying to avoid work—it's more productive to start by trying to learn more. You might begin with a simple request for facts: "What's going on here?" Or, make an observation followed by a question: "Looks like you need some help. Do you want to talk about it now or take a few minutes to cool off?"

One question that's not very helpful to ask children in the moment is "Why?": "Why did you tear up his paper?" "Why did you jab Mike?" "Why are you pounding on your desk?" In the heat of the moment, this question, even if well-intentioned, will sound accusatory to children and make them defensive. Often, the children's response will be to quickly blame the other person or to say blankly, "I don't know." And in many cases, they honestly don't.

The first step in responding to misbehavior is to stop the misbehavior. This sounds obvious, but so often teachers skip this step. Children need to hear the message "Stop now" to break the momentum of their running, yelling, teasing, etc., and change course. To do this, we need to observe children carefully in order to see and consistently respond to small misbehaviors before they become more entrenched patterns.

Simple strategies such as teacher language (see pages 20–27), visual and verbal cues (see pages 68–69), and teacher proximity (see page 69) are useful tools in these instances.

> We need to consistently respond to small misbehaviors before they become more entrenched patterns.

It's in the spirit of maintaining a safe learning environment, preserving children's dignity, and helping them learn from their mistakes—rather than punishing them or making them pay for their mistakes—that the strategies in this chapter are offered.

Using Logical Consequences

In addition to stopping misbehavior, logical consequences are a way of helping children see the connection between their behavior and the effect it has on others. They help children understand that we are all responsible for the consequences of our actions.

It's important to understand the differences between logical consequences and punishment. The two approaches to discipline differ in both intent and application.

	Punishment	Logical Consequences
Intention	To ensure compliance by using external controls that make the child feel ashamed or bad in other ways	To help children recognize the effects of their actions and develop internal controls
Underlying belief	Children will do better only because they fear punishment and will seek to avoid it	Children want to do better and can do better with reflection and practice
Teacher's approach and tone	Reacts automatically with little thought; voice is angry and punitive	Gathers more information before reacting; voice is calm and matter-of-fact
Nature of the consequence	Not related to the behavior or the damage done; not reasonable for the child to do	Related to the behavior; reasonable for the child to do
Message to the child	The child is the problem	The damage done, not the child, is the problem

Unlike punishment, logical consequences are:

- **Respectful**—A logical consequence is communicated in a way that is firm but caring and focuses on the specific behavior rather than making general judgments about the child's character. For example, when issuing a logical consequence to a student who has pushed a classmate, you might say, "Stop. Hands off. Our rules say to treat each other with respect" rather than "Stop being such a bully."

- **Related**—The consequence is directly related to the child's action. For example, if a group of children ask to work together on a project and then use the time to talk about their weekend plans, a related consequence would be that they lose the opportunity to work together that day.

- **Realistic**—The consequence must be something that is realistic for the child to do and for you to follow through on. For example, a logical consequence for a child who writes on a desk is for the child to clean that desk. In contrast, asking the child to clean all the desks in the room would be a disproportionate response and would be very time-consuming, both for the child to complete and for you to monitor.

These guidelines go a long way toward keeping responses to misbehavior nonpunitive. But there is no question that even with the most thoughtful use of logical consequences, children will sometimes protest or resist. They may deny any wrongdoing or complain, "You're always picking on me." It can be a painful and difficult process for children to recognize and take responsibility for their mistakes, as it can be for adults.

It's important for us to remember that we can't control how children feel. Often, children feel bad simply for having made a mistake, lost their self-control, or attracted negative attention. Their protests may be as much a sign of these feelings about themselves as their feelings about our response. It is our job as teachers to help students fix their mistakes and get back on task without further embarrassment.

Three Types of Logical Consequences

There are three basic types of logical consequences: break it, fix it; loss of privilege; and time-out. While there are significant variations in what each looks like at different grade levels, generally, all logical consequences fall within one of these categories.

Break it, fix it—This is as simple and clear as it sounds. If children break something or make a mess, whether intentionally or not, we help them take responsibility for fixing it or cleaning it up. If you jiggle the table and spill the paint, you clean up the table. If you knock someone down on the playing field, you help her up, ask if she's okay, and go with her to the first aid office, if needed.

Loss of privilege—Rather than being a reward for finishing work, a privilege is an opportunity to learn to be reliable and to take responsibility for following the rules when acting autonomously. If a student has trouble responsibly managing a privilege, such as choosing whom to sit next to, the logical consequence is to remove that privilege, say by designating a seat for them for the day. If a student uses a watercolor brush in a way that damages the bristles, he might not be able to choose watercolors as an option during choice time until he's had a chance to practice correct use of the brush and has demonstrated his understanding to you. A key part of this logical consequence is communicating that the privilege is not lost forever—the student will have a chance to try again tomorrow or after they have demonstrated their readiness to handle the responsibility. The goal is for children to show that they can be responsible, not to suffer for being irresponsible.

> It is our job as teachers to help students fix their mistakes and get back on task.

A Word About Time-Out

Because children may have experienced punitive uses of time-out, it's important to explain clearly that the purpose of time-out in this classroom is not to punish anyone but rather to give children a chance to calm down and get back in control so that they can focus on learning. It's important to let students know that after they calm down, they will be welcomed back into the group. You can help remove the stigma surrounding time-out by letting students know that sometimes, they might decide for themselves when they need to take one. In addition, you might choose to call time-out by a different name, such as "take-a-break" or "rest stop." Children, especially in the older grades, may enjoy helping to come up with an appropriate term to use.

It's also key to make sure that while time-out is designed to give children space to calm down, it doesn't make them feel isolated from the rest of the class. There should be one or two designated time-out places in the room—perhaps a chair, a cushion, or a beanbag—that are neither too far away nor in the thick of activity. This gives children the separation they need in order to calm down, yet allows them to keep track of what's going on in the classroom so that they can join in the work when they come back. To keep the child safe, the teacher needs to be able to see the time-out area from anywhere in the room. (See "Teaching Time-Out" on pages 84–87.)

Time-out—This strategy aims to help children learn self-control while keeping the classroom calm, safe, and orderly. A child who is disrupting the work of the group or who is too unfocused or frustrated to learn productively is directed to go to a designated time-out area for a minute or two. During this time, the child is expected to regain self-control so they can come back to the group and participate in a positive way. In some cases, children themselves can decide to go to the time-out spot because they feel themselves losing control and need to leave the scene for a while to regain composure.

Introducing Logical Consequences to Students

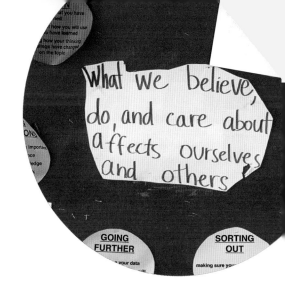

In opening a conversation about logical consequences, you might start by asking questions like "Why is it sometimes hard to follow the rules?" "What's an example of a time you didn't follow the rules?" "How did you feel?" "How do you feel when you are following the rules?" In these conversations, it's important to convey the following messages:

- We are all working together on learning to follow the rules.

- Following the rules takes lots of practice.

- Everyone makes mistakes. We all forget or choose not to follow rules from time to time.

- When someone forgets or chooses not to follow a rule, it's the teacher's job to help that person get back on task and learn to do better next time.

In introducing the concept of logical consequences to students, you might choose to use the actual term "logical consequences." If you do use the term, it's important to define it as a way to solve problems, get back on task, and learn. Ms. Meehan uses the term with her fourth grade class and spends time discussing each word with her students. She uses low-stakes examples from fiction and real life to help students understand cause and effect: If you go outside without an umbrella when it's raining, you'll get wet. That's a natural consequence. "Logical" means related, so a logical consequence is the related result of a student's behavior. For example, if a student knocks a stack of papers onto the floor, they will pick the papers up and help put things back in order so everyone can keep learning. This type of conversation helps students understand the difference between "punishment" and "consequences."

In other cases, such as with younger students, it may be better to keep the terminology simpler. For example, you might begin by saying, "We're all working on following our rules. Let's think for a minute about what happens when we follow our rules." You might give some specific examples of rule following (letting everyone join an activity, working hard with a partner even if they're not your best friend, cleaning the paintbrushes carefully after using them) and then talk with children about the positive consequences of these actions.

Next, you might say, "We all make mistakes from time to time. Sometimes we might forget a rule, or sometimes we might choose not to follow one. What happens when we don't follow a rule—for example, the rules we just talked about?" You can now guide children in thinking about the possible problems that might result, including safety risks, hurt feelings, work left undone, and others' inability to do their work.

> Children will feel more comfortable and assured when they know what the boundaries are and what will happen if those boundaries are crossed.

"In our classroom," you might continue, "when students don't follow a rule, it will be my job to help them get back on task. I'll also help them fix any problems they created and learn to follow the rule next time."

Whether or not you use the term "logical consequences" with students, what's important is to give examples of what those consequences look like. You might say, for instance, "A student is running in the classroom and accidentally knocks over another student's diorama. If that happens, I might tell the person who was running to help repair the damage to the diorama."

Or, "If we're using the staplers for an art project and someone is using a stapler in an unsafe way, I might tell that person to stop using the stapler for the rest of the activity. They could try again next time, and I'll watch to help them make sure they're using it safely."

By giving several concrete examples, you let students know ahead of time what sorts of things will happen when they don't follow the rules. Children will feel more comfortable and assured when they know what the boundaries are and what will happen if those boundaries are crossed. Students will know that you expect them to live by the rules, and that if they don't, you will help them stay safe physically and emotionally and learn to do better next time.

 IN THE CLASSROOM

Logical Consequences

Ms. Meehan, Grade 4 • When introducing logical consequences to students, it's essential to emphasize that nobody's perfect, that everyone makes mistakes, and that learning from one's mistakes is an important part of school. Ms. Meehan is especially careful when teaching her perfectionistic fourth graders about break it, fix it, starting with simple, low-stakes examples like "If you drop a pencil, pick it up." Keeping a relaxed attitude and not showing annoyance when teaching and using break it, fix it helps students understand that while everyone tries their best to take care of their materials, things will get broken or messed up—it's how they deal with their mistakes that matters. It's all part of school, and it's okay.

Ms. Ghosh, Grade 2 • Ms. Ghosh makes sure her students know that even if something is an accident, they still need to fix it. In fact, accidents offer a good way to teach break it, fix it in a low-risk manner—if you spill something, clean it up. Later in the year, she talks with her class about how to "fix it" in social situations, using the language they've already learned to help them think about making amends for hurt or "broken" feelings—for example, asking someone to play at recess if you previously left them out.

Mr. Hunter, Grade 5 • When introducing logical consequences to his students, Mr. Hunter connects the idea to academics. His first science unit of the year is on physics, so he talks about Newton's third law: for every action, there is an equal and opposite reaction. If you break it, you fix it. If you're having trouble with a privilege, you temporarily lose the privilege. And anytime he talks about misbehavior, he refers to "making mistakes" as opposed to "breaking rules." He models fixing his own mistakes for students throughout the year, and he also discusses mistakes he made the previous year and how he addressed them.

Teaching Time-Out

With break it, fix it and loss of privilege, we tell the student exactly what to do. In both of these types of logical consequences, the actual consequence will vary based on the circumstances. Time-out, on the other hand, is a set of specific procedures that need to be taught and practiced through Interactive Modeling (see pages 28–31).

Explicitly teaching time-out procedures means talking about, modeling, and practicing how to do the following:

- Going to the time-out spot quickly, quietly, calmly, and promptly

- Regaining self-control while in time-out without distracting the class (using techniques such as deep breathing or squeezing a stress ball)

- Coming back from time-out quietly and rejoining the work of the group

- Staying focused when a classmate is sent to time-out by leaving the classmate alone

- Going on with the classroom activity while the classmate is in time-out, and welcoming them back when they return

Be sure to practice these procedures with students of all ages. Older students may need less practice, but they may enjoy sharing ideas for how to pull themselves together while in time-out.

When teaching time-out procedures, be sure to clarify who decides when the child should return. The ultimate goal is for children to be able to tell when they're in control and ready to come back. To reach that goal, you might need to explicitly teach children how to use a sand timer to stay in time-out for a particular length of time, or to recognize when they're back in control by listening to the signals from their mind and body. Until you feel that the majority of children are ready for the responsibility of knowing when to return from time-out, you can make that decision. Keep allowing them opportunities to practice recognizing when they're ready to come back. Even when you feel children are ready to come back on their own, there might be times when a child either returns from time-out before having regained control or lingers longer than necessary. In these cases, you can take over the decision for that child the next time.

IN THE CLASSROOM

Time-Out

Mr. Wade, Grade 3 ● "A consequence is a gift I can give you," Mr. Wade tells his students, because it is a way of keeping them on target to achieve their hopes and dreams. After using Interactive Modeling to teach students how to go to take-a-break, he posts an "I took a break" chart and puts up sticky notes with students' names on them, moving each name to the other side of the chart once they've taken a practice break. Mr. Wade also pays close attention to when students go to take-a-break so he can look for patterns and discover potential causes of recurring behavior challenges—for example, whether difficulty focusing during class might actually be related to a struggle with a particular academic subject.

Ms. Meehan, Grade 4 ● When teaching time-out, Ms. Meehan provides ample opportunities for practice. In the first few weeks of school, she makes a point to send each student to time-out twice in order to break the stigma. This works so well that students may start to feel left out if their turn hasn't come up yet!

Mrs. Badge, Grade K ● Mrs. Badge explains to her students that take-a-break is a place for them to get themselves ready to come back to the group. She gives examples of when someone might need to go to take-a-break: "Sometimes, when I'm sitting with my friends, I have a hard time keeping my hands still and paying attention." She uses Interactive Modeling to show children how to go to the take-a-break chair, as well as how to do deep breathing and other techniques for cooling down. She also gives each child the opportunity to practice going to take-a-break.

Ms. Ghosh, Grade 2 ● Ms. Ghosh frequently refers to "privacy" to explain the purpose of time-out ("to get some privacy so you can cool down") and to help the rest of the class understand how to treat a classmate who has been sent to time-out ("give them some privacy"). Understanding this concept also helps children behave respectfully if a student from a different class is having an outburst or is going through some other difficulty in the cafeteria or the hall ("We need to give them some privacy"). Ms. Ghosh also lets her students approach her later on if they're uncertain why they were sent to time-out. She explains what she saw that prompted her to send them, and if the situation wasn't what she thought, she acknowledges the misunderstanding—but reinforces that they did a good job in the moment following the rules and going to time-out without question.

Mr. Hunter, Grade 5 ● Time-out can be a sensitive topic, so Mr. Hunter introduces it a little differently than he does other logical consequences. As a basketball fan, he uses the sport as an example of how taking a break can help a player perform better. If the star player is doing well in a game but comes back after halftime and starts getting cocky and missing shots, what should the coach do? "Call time-out!" responds the class. Why? "Because he's not paying attention or giving his best effort." Why not just have him leave the stadium? "Because he's a good player and he just needs to get back on track." Mr. Hunter tells his students that in this class, everyone is a star player, and we all sometimes need to pause, take a breath, make adjustments, and come back in. Time-out is an opportunity to be the best player you can be.

Here are some additional guidelines for teachers when using time-out:

- **Use time-out just as a child is beginning to lose control.** Don't wait until the behavior has escalated and the child has lost face with peers. Using time-out early helps preserve children's relationships and the teacher's feelings of empathy. It can be tough, for example, to feel empathy when a child has become aggressive. If a child has progressed to being fully out of control, you need another strategy, perhaps one that involves the principal, a guidance counselor, or other support staff.

- **Use a calm, quiet voice to tell a child to go to time-out.** Or, when possible, use a visual signal to give this direction. This avoids drawing attention to the child.

- **Keep instructions to go to time-out simple and nonnegotiable.** An important purpose of time-out is to allow the work of the group to go on when a student is misbehaving. Discussing the situation with the student will only disrupt the group further. Moreover, the student is usually not in a frame of mind at the moment to discuss the situation reasonably. However, when introducing time-out, it's important to assure students that they can always talk with you about the situation later.

- **Use time-out for everyone.** At one point or another, almost all children in a classroom lose their cool or their focus and can use a method to collect themselves. It's important that students see that time-out is used for anyone and everyone who needs it and not just the same two or three children.

> At one point or another, almost all children in a classroom lose their cool or their focus and can use a method to collect themselves.

- **Allow students to send themselves to time-out, if appropriate.** If students are older or if it's later in the year and time-out is well established, you may also choose to allow students to send themselves to time-out if they feel they need to calm down. This is another way of emphasizing that time-out is not a punishment but an opportunity to regain self-control. You can even send yourself when you're feeling stressed out to model the behavior of cooling down and getting back in control of yourself.

- **Have a system for time-out in another room.** Many teachers set up a "buddy teacher" system for times when a student refuses to go to time-out, continues to be disruptive in time-out, or continues to be disruptive after coming back from time-out. In those cases, you can have the child take a time-out in the buddy teacher's room. This prevents the situation from escalating into a power struggle and allows you to go on teaching the class. (See the following section for more information on working with a buddy teacher.)

- **Remember that time-out does not work in some cases.** If you send a child to time-out over and over without seeing any improvement in behavior, or if a child crumbles or becomes extremely distraught at even one use of time-out, it's more than likely the child needs a different strategy. Chapters 4 and 5 cover alternative strategies for responding to misbehavior that is ongoing or the result of toxic stress.

Buddy Teacher Time-Out

When a child needs a longer break or needs to leave the classroom in order to regain control of their behavior, you can send them to time-out in a buddy teacher's classroom. Buddy teacher time-out can be useful for situations when regular time-out has not stopped the behavior, the child is disrupting others in the class or feeding off of their attention while in time-out, or the child is too upset or angry to calm down within your classroom space. Buddy teacher time-out is also useful for students who become too self-conscious in regular time-out for it to be effective.

IN THE CLASSROOM

Buddy Teacher Time-Out

Mrs. Badge, Grade K ● When Mrs. Badge and her teaching partner use buddy teacher time-out, they know it may be slightly different each time, depending on the student and situation. For some children, going to a different classroom is enough to help them reset their behavior, and they're able to participate with the buddy teacher's class for a little while. Other students may simply need to take time-out in the buddy teacher's classroom if participating is disruptive to the class or isn't helping the child calm down. Each child is unique, and what they need depends on their state of mind in the moment.

If students are developmentally ready and the situation is appropriate, you might send them on their own to the buddy teacher's room to sit in the time-out area there. In other cases, you can send a pre-established signal to summon the buddy teacher while you continue teaching or dealing with an outburst in your own room. For example, you could have a different student or a paraprofessional go to the buddy teacher's classroom and give a hand signal or hold up a red pen.

It's helpful to identify one or more buddy teachers early in the year and plan together how to use these strategies. And as with regular time-out, it's important to explain the purpose of buddy teacher time-out to your students, and to teach procedures for going, staying, and returning. It's also important to discuss, model, and practice how other children should behave when a classmate goes to buddy teacher time-out, when they return, and when someone from the buddy teacher's class comes to take time-out in your room.

Additional Tips

When using logical consequences, here are a few other considerations to keep in mind.

The Teacher Decides on the Consequence

Choosing a logical consequence is not a collaborative process. When introducing logical consequences, you may ask children to come up with some appropriate consequences for various hypothetical situations. Such a discussion can help children understand the intention and characteristics of this way of handling rule breaking. In actual rule-breaking situations, however, you are in charge of deciding on the consequence.

Choosing an appropriate logical consequence is a complex decision requiring knowledge and mature judgment. Most elementary school students have a difficult time distinguishing between logical consequences and punishments. Asked to decide on a logical consequence for themselves, students are likely to dole out harsh punishments and judgments. Deciding on logical consequences for other students is not a position elementary school students should ever be in.

Additional Tips for Using Logical Consequences

The teacher decides on the consequence

One size does not fit all

Have preset consequences for certain situations

If it doesn't seem obvious, it's probably not logical

Sometimes two steps are needed

Keep explanations brief

Rely on colleagues for help

Have a reentry check-in if a child must leave the room

Try, try again

One Size Does Not Fit All

Each child—and situation—is unique, and different situations call for different responses. When children misbehave, they offer valuable information about what they need.

In *Maintaining Sanity in the Classroom* (1982), Dreikurs, Grunwald, and Pepper write about the need that all people have for a sense of belonging and a sense of importance, or significance. Researcher Edward Deci (1995) frames these fundamental human needs as the need for autonomy (the freedom to control oneself), relatedness (being connected to others), and competence (the ability to achieve desired outcomes). Both Dreikurs et al. and Deci remind us that when people's basic psychological needs are not met, they often act out in negative ways. Understanding what's behind a child's misbehavior can help you choose an effective response.

Here are a few questions you might ask when a child misbehaves:

- Are expectations clear? Too high? Too low?
- Is this behavior part of a pattern? Or is it an isolated incident?
- Is the child testing the limits? Engaging in a power struggle?
- What's been helpful for this child in the past? What hasn't been helpful?

The same behavior may demand very different logical consequences with different children, since what's motivating each child and what each child understands determine what that child needs to learn and what problem needs to be fixed. The point is not to apply consequences uniformly, but to understand where each child is coming from and choose a consequence that makes sense for that child. We build trust with our students by being consistent in our response to misbehavior, but consistency comes from always intervening when a student exhibits a misbehavior—regardless of who the student is, what the action is, or what logical consequence is required.

Have Preset Consequences for Certain Situations

Although each situation is unique, there are times—particularly when safety is a concern—when a preset response is justified. For example, you might decide that any child who runs in the hallway would, for a period of time, have to be accompanied when leaving the classroom. Each teacher should decide what situations require such nonnegotiable, preset consequences.

If It Doesn't Seem Obvious, It's Probably Not Logical

In making sure that logical consequences are, indeed, logical, the key is to look at each situation and ask, "What's the problem here? Hurt feelings? A safety issue? Distraction from work? Disturbing others? How can I stop the problematic action? And, given what I know about this child and these circumstances, how can I help this child see and fix the problem?" If the consequence doesn't become obvious after this reflection, then it's quite likely that the situation requires something other than a logical consequence. We can still respond in a way that is respectful, related, realistic, and nonpunitive. It's also possible that, in this particular situation, no imposed consequence is needed. If a child forgets to bring home a permission form to get signed and therefore cannot participate in a field trip or a photo-taking session, not being able to take part is itself a significant enough consequence that it no doubt teaches the child a great deal about taking responsibility. In that case, there's no need to impose a further consequence.

> Understanding what's behind a child's misbehavior can help you choose an effective response.

Sometimes Two Steps Are Needed

There are times when we can get so angry and frustrated that we can't think clearly. In times like these, when emotions obscure logic, the best thing for us to do is respectfully stop the misbehavior in the moment (for example, removing the child from the situation by sending them to buddy teacher time-out). Later, after everyone has had time to cool off, you can decide if any further action is needed. You might set up a time to talk with the child after lunch, after recess, or at some later point in the day. Keep in mind, however, that this waiting time can be a great source of anxiety for some children. If this might be the case for a particular child, keep the cool-off period as short as possible.

Many teachers recognize that during these times of anger and frustration, they themselves need a time-out. You can call on a colleague to be with your class for a few minutes while you take a walk down the hall. If this isn't possible, you might change the class activity so that students are working independently. You can then sit quietly at your desk for a few minutes.

If the consequence is well chosen, it will be more powerful than any words.

Keep Explanations Brief

When using a logical consequence, the less said, the better. Let the consequence do the job. If the consequence is well chosen, it will be more powerful than any words. Additional explanations can easily undermine that power and exacerbate any classroom disruption that the child's behavior may have caused.

Rely on Colleagues for Help

Beyond setting up a buddy teacher system (see pages 87–88), there are informal ways for teachers to get crucial support from each other. If the same behavior problem keeps showing up in your classroom or if a particular child makes you especially angry or frustrated, talk with colleagues about it. Often, good solutions emerge from the collective experience and wisdom of teachers and staff.

Have a Reentry Check-In if a Child Must Leave the Room

If the logical consequence involves the child leaving the room—to go to a buddy teacher's room or to the principal's office, for example—it's crucial to check in with the child before bringing them back into the classroom. The conversation will be about what happened, what needs to be done now, and how to prevent similar situations in the future. Taking the time for this step reassures you that the child is ready to come back to the class. It also shows the child that they are still liked and respected and that relationships are intact.

Try, Try Again

Responding to misbehavior is challenging—perhaps one of the most challenging aspects of teaching. Even the most experienced teachers make mistakes. But the most experienced teachers will also be the first to say that we must allow ourselves to make mistakes, just as we allow students to make them. And just as we tell our students—without shaming them—to "try, try again," we must allow ourselves to try again without self-defeating judgments, but with the spirit of learning to do better next time. As Dreikurs et al. (1982) point out, it's not the mistake, but what one does about it, that's important. In time, mistakes will give way to successes.

 To learn more strategies for responding to a variety of specific misbehaviors, see *Teasing, Tattling, Defiance and More: Positive Approaches to 10 Common Classroom Behaviors* by Margaret Berry Wilson (Center for Responsive Schools, 2013).

CHAPTER SUMMARY

Responding to Misbehavior

1 Children have many reasons for misbehaving, and are still in the early stages of learning the rules of the world.

2 The goals when responding to misbehavior are to stop the negative behavior, reestablish positive behavior quickly so the child can return to learning, and help them learn from their mistakes.

3 Logical consequences differ from punishment in that they are respectful, related, and realistic.

4 There are three types of logical consequences teachers can use: break it, fix it; loss of privilege; and time-out, all of which are intended to stop misbehavior and help students regain control and get back to learning.

5 Teachers should remember that each situation is different, and each child is unique and deserving of empathy.

References

Deci, Edward L. (with Richard Flaste). 1995. *Why We Do What We Do.* New York: Penguin.

Dreikurs, Rudolf, Bernice Bronia Grunwald, and Floy C. Pepper. 1982. *Maintaining Sanity in the Classroom: Classroom Management Techniques.* 2nd ed. New York: Harper and Row.

MacKenzie, Robert J. 1997. "Setting Limits in the Classroom." *American Educator* 21 (3): 32–43.

Solving Problem Behavior

Solving Problem Behavior

W hile logical consequences are an effective way to respond to many types of misbehaviors, some students need additional support to build good self-control and follow the rules on a consistent basis. The previous chapter covered common misbehavior, which all children exhibit from time to time. Problem behavior is a different phenomenon and refers to an ongoing pattern in which a student continues to struggle with a particular behavior challenge.

Logical consequences are meant to be used when an individual incident of common misbehavior occurs, but if a student or an entire class is struggling with problem behavior, additional strategies may be useful. Whether a child keeps doodling instead of working on assignments, a student frequently gets too rambunctious when walking in the halls, or a whole class is regularly having side conversations during group discussions, the ideas in this chapter may provide solutions.

The strategies outlined here rely on collaboration. They bring teachers and students together in the interest of helping students do well in school and establish healthy relationships with others. These strategies focus on finding customized ways to help students learn the skills they need to follow the rules, and aim for realistic improvement in behavior.

And remember, true collaboration can only happen when empathy is present. It is essential to show empathy toward students who exhibit problem behavior, as challenging as that may sometimes be. Try not to take problem behavior personally, and keep in mind that some students need a little more help than others to follow the rules, just as some students need individualized attention in math or reading. Think of positive behavior as another subject to be taught, and consider the techniques in this chapter as additional learning strategies that can help.

Checking the Foundations of Good Behavior

Before moving beyond logical consequences—especially if multiple students are exhibiting a particular type of problem behavior—take some time to assess whether the class needs a refresher on the rules and routines. Maybe it's partway through the year, and it's been a while since you last had a discussion about what the classroom rule "Take care of others" looks, sounds, and feels like in action. Maybe students need to be reminded through Interactive Modeling or role-playing how to respond to the signal for quiet or politely ask a tablemate to share materials. Some students may need more discussion and practice than others to really understand the rules and routines.

It may be helpful to assess yourself, too. Check your use of teacher language: Are you consistently and effectively using envisioning, reinforcing, reminding, and redirecting language? It's also important to ensure that you're using logical consequences consistently, calmly, and at the first sign of behavior going off task. If students learn that they can get away with a misbehavior some of the time, logical consequences may be less of a deterrent.

And of course, be sure to think about children's basic needs. Do students tend to argue more each day around midmorning when they're hungry? Maybe an earlier snack time would help. Does daydreaming and doodling increase when students have been sitting still for a long lesson? Maybe they could use a few more energizers throughout the day (see pages 124–125). Have students recently been having a harder time working together in groups? Maybe they have reached a new developmental phase where working with a single partner would be more productive. Are their needs for belonging, significance, and fun being met? Maybe it's time to change up your lesson plans and activities. Look for patterns and think about whether students' physical, social, and developmental needs are being met.

Once you've established that students have what they need and understand what's expected of them—and that you're following through as needed when they don't meet those expectations—it may be time to move on to other strategies if behavior still doesn't improve:

- Problem-solving conferences for individual students who are exhibiting an ongoing problem behavior

- Individual written agreements for students who require more intense structure, feedback, and incentives to change their behavior

- Structured class meetings for a whole group that is struggling with a particular issue

Whichever strategies you use, remember that it's a sign of strength, not weakness, to seek advice from and collaborate with other teachers and experts in your school, such as counselors, the special education team, and social workers. These colleagues may be able to provide information to help you better understand your students and find the most effective ways to help them with their behavior. Your colleagues can also help you practice the strategies outlined in this chapter so that you'll be ready to implement them with confidence in your classroom.

IN THE CLASSROOM

Assessing Students' Needs

Mr. Wade, Grade 3 ● If a chronic or classwide behavior challenge is occurring, Mr. Wade starts by asking himself what's going on and what he can improve upon. Is instruction engaging enough? Is the environment safe and welcoming? He also asks individual students who are struggling what they need in order to stay on task, and he then tries to proactively give them what they need.

Ms. Meehan, Grade 4 ● In order to treat students fairly, we sometimes need to treat them differently. If logical consequences aren't proving effective with a student, Ms. Meehan may quietly say to them, "I can tell you need something. After you calm down, we can talk about it." This helps her get to know her students, helps her figure out what will improve their behavior, and helps the students understand that she wants to help them.

Ms. Ghosh, Grade 2 ● Ms. Ghosh finds that when a whole class is having issues with a particular behavior challenge, it's helpful to go through the full process of Interactive Modeling again, or to do another round of role-playing if the problem is a social one. She also makes a point to refer back to the rules frequently and to have students reflect on how they're doing following the rules after an incident occurs.

Mr. Hunter, Grade 5 ● Some children really need a lot of physical activity. When these students start to have trouble staying focused, Mr. Hunter has them take a walk to a specific place (like the water fountain or cafeteria) and back. Or, he might send a student to run an errand around the school, which gives them the opportunity to "walk it off" and feels to the child like being useful rather than being kicked out of class.

Mrs. Badge, Grade K ● Running errands also works for students who just need to leave the room for a few minutes in order to calm down. Mrs. Badge had one student like this, and would give her a note to take to the school administrative assistant when the student struggled to get control of herself. The note might simply say "Let her sit here for five or ten minutes," and when the administrative assistant received it, she would say, "Okay, have a seat and I'll be with you in a few minutes." After the time had elapsed, she would give the child a note to bring back to the classroom that said "All okay" or had the time written on it. The student felt like she'd accomplished something, and she'd had a chance to calm down.

Problem-Solving Conferences

For some students, problem behavior can be addressed with individual supports such as private signals or reminders, scheduled breaks, or different ways of getting schoolwork done. For example, a child who struggles with talking too much during discussions might get a special hand signal from the teacher to help them know it's time to give others a chance to speak. Or a student who routinely daydreams during math lessons might need a little private instruction time or different learning tools. Problem-solving conferences offer students and teachers the opportunity to work together to come up with these sorts of solutions.

A problem-solving conference is a private, one-on-one discussion between a teacher and a student that allows both parties to discuss one specific problem behavior, identify its possible causes, and brainstorm potential solutions. By giving the student a voice, you are able to learn about what's really going on with the child, who often has insights into their own behaviors and needs that you may not yet know. The conference should take 10 to 15 minutes and may be scheduled before or after school, as a private lunch, or while a colleague supervises the rest of the class.

> By giving the student a voice, you are able to learn about what's really going on with the child, who often has insights into their own behaviors.

Before meeting with the student, plan out the conference and brainstorm some potential causes of the behavior and some solutions to try. However, be sure to allow the student the opportunity to offer their own suggestions as well as react to yours. As with the other techniques outlined in this book, keeping teacher talk to a minimum will help the student focus and understand what you're trying to say. It will also leave space for them to express their feelings and know that their voice is important, too.

In addition to your own knowledge about the student, their needs, and their developmental stage, it may help to bring outside information to a problem-solving conference. Talk to colleagues who know the child and find out what insights they might have. And parents, of course, can provide a wealth of information about their child's home life, friendships, background, and any issues that might influence their ability to do well in school.

Use the following steps to help you run effective problem-solving conferences.

1 **Tell the student what you want to talk about, and set a time to meet.** You might say, "I'd like to talk to you about some things I've noticed during reading time. Would you like to have lunch with me in the classroom today?" Choosing a time the student agrees to will help you start off on the right foot. For example, if the student was looking forward to talking to their best friend at lunch about last night's baseball game, you might choose instead to meet in the afternoon during choice time. Also, make sure to allow enough time between an occurrence of the problem behavior and the meeting time so that both you and the student have enough distance to think clearly about the issue. For example, if the behavior is happening during reading time and reading time is right before lunch, then you should probably plan the conference for a different time.

2 **Establish the purpose of the conference.** When you do sit down to begin the conference, start by reiterating what you'd like to discuss with the student: "I'm glad we're meeting so we can talk about how things are going during reading time." If they bring up other issues they're having, be clear that today, you're only going to talk about the one specific thing you mentioned.

3 **Start with the positive.** It's essential to build a positive relationship with children before having a problem-solving conference with them, and to affirm your rapport as the conference begins. Letting the student know you've noticed a recent accomplishment of theirs helps them feel that you like them and are on their side. This sets the stage for a strong collaboration between the two of you. Look for accomplishments related to the area you'll be discussing in the conference so that the student knows you have faith in their ability to succeed: "I have noticed in reading that you have a lot of strategies to sound out new words and are able to quickly learn how to say those words! Tell me about some of your strategies."

4 **State the problem.** Be specific and brief so that you clearly communicate the issue to the student. Also, keep an objective tone and stay focused on the facts of the behavior rather than on placing judgment or assigning blame. For example: "I've noticed you often whisper to others during individual reading." Then, ask the student what they have noticed. Maybe they have noticed the issue before, too, or maybe this is the first time they're becoming aware of it. Either way, it's important that you both agree the issue is happening before trying to address it. If the student doesn't see their behavior as a problem, the problem-solving conference isn't the right approach to change it. Instead, be extra clear about classroom rules, and redouble your efforts with using logical consequences.

5 **Discuss why it's important to solve the problem.** Talk about why the behavior is problematic, how it doesn't follow the class rules, and the ways that it may negatively affect the student and others. For example: "When you whisper during reading time, you're not following our rules to take care of our learning and each other. Whispering keeps you from getting your own reading done and it distracts others." Then confirm with the student that they want to work on the issue together. If they aren't willing to collaborate, you may need to think about ways to build a stronger relationship with them before trying problem-solving conferences.

6 **Talk about what might be causing the problem.** Might the student be whispering during reading time because they're picking books that are too hard or too easy for them and are having trouble staying focused? Could it be that they're struggling with reading and are looking to others for help? Suggest a couple of ideas and ask the student if they seem true, and then see if the student has other ideas. They may surprise you with a cause you hadn't considered—for example, "I never get to hang out with Adrienne and Priya since my family moved across town. We always used to talk about our books together on the bus, but now I take a different bus."

7 **Set a clear, specific goal to work on together.** For some problem behaviors, there may be single goal for the student to work toward, such as staying focused and quiet during reading time. With other behaviors, there might be multiple goals. For example, a student struggling with silliness during Morning Meeting might need to stay seated, keep quiet while others are speaking, make sincere comments after others share, and find a different outlet to express their sense of humor. Choose a single goal to work on at first, and state that goal in a positive way using envisioning language: "Dani will stay focused on her own book during reading time."

8 **Brainstorm solutions to try.** Once you and the student have identified the likely cause of the problem behavior and set a goal, talk about possible strategies for reaching that goal. Again, you can think of a few ideas in advance, but be prepared to adjust them if the root of the behavior is different than you thought. And be sure to ask if the student has ideas for strategies, too. "Maybe you and your friends could talk about your books at recess," you might suggest. Or the student might say, "Maybe we could have a book club during choice time." Weed out any impractical solutions (such as letting the friends read together instead of doing social studies lessons).

9 **Select one strategy to try first.** Ask which of the brainstormed strategies the student would like to start with. "Maybe I'll try talking about our books at recess." Discuss how you'll both know whether the strategy is working.

10 **Follow up.** One of the most easily overlooked steps—but an essential one—is to follow up after the conference to see how things are going. As part of the initial conference, set a date for a check-in meeting to assess how the strategy is working and whether a different one needs to be tried. Reinforce any progress the student has made.

Problem-Solving Conferences

Mrs. Badge, Grade K • With her kindergartners, Mrs. Badge holds simple, one-on-one conversations to talk about what's going on. She asks, "What could you do next time?" These discussions help prepare young students for the full process of problem-solving conferences.

Mr. Hunter, Grade 5 • In problem-solving conferences, Mr. Hunter recognizes the value of asking a student's permission to help them with a problem behavior in order to reinforce the student's agency and autonomy. In an adult-centric world, asking "Have you noticed . . . ?" and "Would you like help working on that?" can work like magic to help students open up.

Ms. Ghosh, Grade 2 • Ms. Ghosh emphasizes the importance of following up with students after holding a problem-solving conference with them. She makes sure her students have a say in setting their own goals and determining when they've reached them. If a student is consistently meeting a goal they've set during a problem-solving conference, she follows up again to help them set a new one, if needed.

Ms. Meehan, Grade 4 • Ms. Meehan makes a point of letting her fourth graders talk first in problem-solving conferences. She asks, "What have you noticed that's preventing you from doing your best learning?" If students reply, "I don't know," Ms. Meehan often uses this trick: "If you did know, what would you say?" This question acts as a sort of key that unlocks students' thinking by letting them take a mental step back from the problem to see it more clearly.

Individual Written Agreements

Some students require highly structured support to break nonproductive habits and build positive ones. An individual written agreement is a way to provide that support. The teacher and student agree on a behavior goal, a way to document the student's success in meeting it, and, if appropriate, a reward for meeting it. Often, when teachers use individual written agreements, they do so with support from parents, behavior specialists, and other adults who are part of the child's life.

Because these agreements are time-intensive and often rely on extrinsic rewards, they should be used sparingly and only after trying other techniques. One of the most important elements of the individual written agreement is the use of frequent reminders and encouragement from the teacher, so it's important to assess whether it's feasible for you to provide this level of feedback. If not, consider whether increasing your efforts with logical consequences or holding additional problem-solving conferences might be more helpful, or if there are any academic or social supports that might help solve the problem. It may also be worthwhile to consult with your school's behavior specialist or other experts on the best ways to help the child learn.

> Some students require highly structured support to break nonproductive habits and build positive ones.

Before meeting with a student about an individual written agreement, take some time to think about why they might be misbehaving and consider possible solutions. Determine the specific behavior you want the student to adopt, consider how you will measure their progress, and think about how you will reinforce positive efforts, including acceptable choices for rewards, if used. You'll also want to contact the student's parents before proceeding to let them know the purpose of the meeting, enlist their support, and get any insights they have to share. Parents are often supportive of individual written agreements and willing to help, as problems you're seeing in the classroom may also be occurring at home, and they, too, may be looking for solutions.

Once you're prepared, consider the following when using an individual written agreement.

- **Set a concrete, measurable goal.** This is an essential piece of the process, as students need a way to understand whether they're behaving according to the teacher's expectations, and the teacher needs an objective way to measure progress. For a student who frequently calls out and interrupts others during class, the goal might be "Olivia will let others finish speaking and then raise her hand and wait to be called on." Strive for progress rather than perfection; the target might be to meet the goal 80 percent of the time.

- **Clearly track the child's progress.** Do this in a visible way, such as with check marks on a chart or craft sticks in a jar, so that the student can see how they're doing. This tracking should happen regularly throughout the day at designated times, such as on an hourly basis or after each subject period. At the end of each interval, if the student has met their goal, give the visible reinforcement you've agreed on. At the same time, offer a verbal reinforcement by telling the child what you noticed. It's essential for the student to get this reinforcement on a regular basis throughout the day (rather than waiting until the end of the day or week) so that they know they're making progress and can more easily stay on track.

- **Use a nontangible reward, if needed.** Some children will derive enough motivation to change their behavior from the visible tracking of their progress and the frequent feedback from the teacher. Other children will benefit from earning an external reward for their progress. As part of the initial agreement you set up with the student, decide whether or not rewards will be given, how frequently, and what those rewards will be. Avoid tangible prizes like toys or snacks, and instead offer a special activity the student will enjoy, such as extra reading time or helping the music teacher set up instruments. If you do use a reward system, be careful to gradually wean the student off of it as they strengthen their good habits. Any external reward, if used for too long, can stand in the way of the student developing their own internal motivation to behave well and contribute to a positive and productive classroom.

Class Meetings

When problem behavior moves beyond a single student or a few individuals, it may be helpful to bring the whole class together in a structured meeting to help solve the problem. Class meetings give everyone in the room a chance to weigh in on the problem, suggest possible solutions, and find a solution on which all members of the class can agree.

A class meeting is a strategy to try when the agreed-on rules aren't working, when the problem affects everyone in the class, and when you're open to student input—for example, if students routinely exclude others on the playground, or if they often neglect to put their materials away neatly and carefully, leaving supply areas in disarray. If a problem only affects a few members of the class, you might try meeting with them individually, and if you aren't open to student input for solving the problem, you might need to use Interactive Modeling to teach or remind students how they should behave in the given situation.

It's also important to consider the developmental stage of your students and whether or not they're ready to take on the full process of class meetings. Will they be able to apply the level of reasoning needed to identify the causes of problem behavior and come up with feasible solutions? Kindergartners and first graders may need a modified class meeting format in which they share what they've noticed and brainstorm possible solutions, but you choose which solution to try. Even older students who are inexperienced in whole-group problem-solving may need extra support as they learn this process.

Follow these steps to run an effective class meeting.

1. **Choose an appropriate meeting time.** Plan for about half an hour for the meeting. It would not be appropriate to hold the meeting during recess or another privileged time because doing so could make the meeting seem like a punishment, and students might then be less invested in participating. Also, if you use the *Responsive Classroom* practice of Morning Meeting, don't try to fit a problem-solving class meeting into that time. Morning Meeting has its own distinct and important purpose that should be honored.

2. **Start on a positive note.** You might ask students to think of ways the class has been doing well in following the rules to help start the discussion out on the right foot.

3 **State the reason for the meeting.** Keep it brief, specific, and nonjudgmental. For instance, you might say, "Today, we're meeting to talk about some things I've noticed when we're working on art projects. Sometimes, I see and hear students not sharing art supplies."

4 **Connect the problem to the class rules.** Remind students of the class rules and how those rules help them meet their learning goals—and how the problem behavior can get in the way of them reaching their goals: "Our class rule says to be kind to everyone. That rule helps us meet our personal goals by showing we support each other in learning. When we don't share supplies with our classmates, we aren't following the rule to be kind. That makes it harder for everyone to meet their goals."

5 **Invite students' input with open-ended questions.** Ask what students have noticed in relation to the issue. Going around the circle, each student may say something they've noticed or how it makes them feel, or they may say "Pass." For example, one student might say that they want to finish what they're doing before they give their supplies to another person, and another student might say, "When I need paints for my project and I can't get them, it makes me mad."

6 **Ask for potential solutions to the problem.** Go around the circle again and let each student propose a solution or say "Pass." Record these ideas as they're suggested. "Maybe everyone could only get two minutes to use a paint color and then the next person gets it." "Maybe different people could pick paints first every day." Finally, allow students to respectfully comment on the ideas that have been proposed, and narrow the list down to a few realistic solutions you'd be comfortable trying.

7 **Choose a solution to try.** For each possible solution, have students vote with thumbs up if they want to try it, thumbs to the side if they can live with it, and thumbs down if they can't live with it. If any of the ideas get any thumbs down, talk about possible compromises or other ideas to try instead. All students in the class need to be able to at least live with an idea to achieve consensus. For example, maybe a student doesn't want a two-minute time limit on using supplies. A second student might suggest, "What if you could use it as long as you want, but if somebody asks for it, you have two minutes to finish using it?" The first student might then be able to live with the solution, and a new vote might show all thumbs up or to the side.

8 **Sum up the plan.** Once consensus has been reached, confirm the plan by restating the solution and recognizing students' efforts in collaborative problem-solving: "We've agreed that if someone else asks to use an item we're using, we will take two minutes to finish up and then pass the item on. The person who asks will turn over a sand timer to keep track of how much time is left. You were all very thoughtful in coming up with ways to share supplies so we can support each other in doing our best learning."

9 **Keep following up.** As students implement the plan the class agreed on, reinforce their efforts and recognize their successes. It may take more than one class meeting to address persistent issues, so if follow-up meetings are needed, have students reflect on what's working and what isn't and refine their ideas about what might help them successfully address the issue.

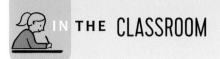

IN THE CLASSROOM

Class Meetings

Ms. Meehan, Grade 4 •
Class or team meetings—or as Ms. Meehan calls them, community meetings—are important because they give everyone a chance to talk and to hear from everyone else in the group. In addition to using these meetings to deal with problem behavior, Ms. Meehan uses them in a proactive way to teach children about ADHD, autism, trauma, and other experiences children in the class may be having. She does this without naming names, often using books or stories to help children develop empathy, but she also invites students (with their parents' consent) to talk about their own experiences if they are comfortable doing so.

Talking to Parents About Problem Behavior

Communicating with parents early and often is key when teaching positive behavior. Not only do parents deserve to know how their child is doing in school, but they can also provide valuable insights to help you better understand the child and more successfully deal with any problem behavior the child might be experiencing.

Here are some tips for creating a strong parent-teacher team as you work to solve behavior problems.

- **Make sure parents know you like their child and see the good in them.** Just as it's essential to establish a strong connection with your students, building rapport with parents is also important. If you're able to talk about the ways in which you truly appreciate and understand a child, you'll earn more trust from their parents. That will help them see, when you bring up challenges with behavior, that you have a genuine interest in helping the child do well. Contacting families regularly with positive updates can also help to overwrite negative associations parents may have with teacher messages. Drop them a note about how their child reached out to a new student, showed a lot of effort on their recent science report, or dazzled the class with their drawings.

- **Get in touch early when problem behavior starts.** If you wait until a minor behavior problem has escalated into a major one, parents may grow angry or frustrated that they didn't hear about it sooner. Contact them as soon as you notice a pattern of problem behavior beginning, and let them know what you've noticed and how you're working with the child to address the problem. In some cases, parents may be able to reinforce your strategies when the child is at home. For example, they might help the child check a weekly planner to stay on top of homework assignments.

- **Stay focused on the facts.** When telling parents about problem behavior their child is experiencing, stay specific and objective. Describe what you're seeing, and avoid judging or labeling the behavior. Parents will be more receptive to hearing "Zack has been expressing his frustration by yelling when other children want to play a different game than he does" than to "Zack is such an angry, oversensitive child."

- **Be clear about how the behavior may hurt the child.** Parents will be more invested in dealing with problem behavior if they understand how that behavior may negatively impact their child socially or academically. For example, you might say, "I'm concerned about Zack expressing his feelings this way because it might make it harder for him to connect with other students and make friends. I want to help him find healthy and productive ways to get what he needs and manage his frustration."

Communicating with parents early and often is key when teaching positive behavior.

- **Know why you're reaching out to parents.** Have a clear purpose when you contact parents so that they understand you aren't blaming them or leaving it up to them to deal with the problem on their own. You might reach out simply to inform parents of what's going on and to let them know what you're working on with their child. You might contact parents to seek insight, particularly if you notice a change in the child's normal behavior and are wondering if something might be going on outside of school. Or, you might want help from parents (if it's realistic for them to give it) to carry out strategies you've worked on with their child, like practicing relaxation techniques with a child who is struggling to manage their anger.

To learn more about the collaborative strategies outlined in this chapter, see *Solving Thorny Behavior Problems: How Teachers and Students Can Work Together* by Caltha Crowe (Center for Responsive Schools, 2009).

Solving Problem Behavior

1 Make sure students have a clear understanding of the expectations and that their needs are being met before moving on to more intensive strategies for dealing with problem behavior.

2 Problem-solving conferences bring the student and teacher together to come up with possible solutions to problem behavior.

3 Individual written agreements offer highly structured support to students who may need additional coaching and reinforcement to reduce negative behaviors and build positive ones.

4 Class meetings let an entire class work together to give everyone a voice and solve problem behavior that affects the whole group.

5 When communicating with parents, be sure to let them know you like their child, get in touch early when issues arise, focus on the facts of the problem behavior and how it may harm the child, and be clear about your purpose in contacting parents.

5

Managing the Effects of Toxic Stress

Managing the Effects of Toxic Stress

For a child experiencing severe stress on an ongoing basis, the world may not always feel logical or predictable. Children from any background can experience this phenomenon, which is known as toxic stress. For example, in a home where one or more parents struggle with addiction, a child might feel that their family is calm and peaceful one day, and chaotic and scary the next. Or a family dealing with the effects of poverty might be able to pay the bills to keep the heat on—until the car suddenly breaks down and they can't. If the world isn't logical to these children, it's understandable that they may react to stimuli in ways that seem illogical to us—and that logical consequences may not always be the right tool to help them.

This chapter explains how toxic stress can influence children's minds and bodies, as well as their lives in the classroom. Being part of a safe, predictable learning community and having consistent relationships with caring adults can make a significant difference for children experiencing toxic stress, and this chapter includes information on how to create those conditions. It also includes strategies for dealing with outbursts and other behavioral results of toxic stress.

Healthy Stress vs. Toxic Stress

According to Harvard University's Center on the Developing Child (n.d.), there are three levels of response to stress that children may experience. Just like adults, all children feel minor to moderate stress sometimes—for example, on the first day at a new school, or if an unfamiliar dog barks at them and scares them. When a child is under stress, their cortisol and other stress hormone levels rise, along with their blood pressure and heart rates. But these levels return to a healthy baseline after the stressful moment has passed. This response is an adaptive mechanism that has helped human beings survive dangerous situations for thousands of years, and experiencing it on this level is part of developing a healthy stress response system.

When stressful events are more extreme, as in the case of a natural disaster or the death of a loved one, the physical and chemical changes the body undergoes can be pushed beyond the healthy stress response. Still, children's bodies and minds can recover from this heightened stress if the event is limited in time and the child has a strong network of positive relationships with adults who can help them cope and feel safe (Changing Minds, n.d.-a).

> When stressful events happen on a regular basis to a child who does not have sufficient support from adults, that child can experience a toxic stress response.

However, when stressful events happen on a regular basis to a child who does not have sufficient support from adults, that child can experience a toxic stress response. This sort of prolonged stress can happen to students from any background, and can result from many causes, including abuse, neglect, a parent's addiction or chronic illness, repeated exposure to violence in the home or community, poverty, systemic discrimination, or other issues. The ongoing uncertainty and danger in this climate of stress keeps children on high alert, making them prone to reacting in "fight, flight, or freeze" mode even in situations where they are not in danger. For example, they might misconstrue a teacher's constructive criticism as a put-down or assume someone who accidentally bumps into them in the hall is starting a fight.

The prolonged presence of elevated stress hormones in the body can harm children's brains and other organs into adulthood, leading to increased long-term risks of physical and mental illnesses such as heart disease, substance abuse, and depression. In addition, elevated stress hormones may damage children's cognitive development, increasing neural connections to parts of the brain associated with anxiety and impulsiveness and diminishing those connected with behavior regulation. Fortunately, healthy relationships with adults can help mitigate these risks, preventing or even reversing some of the damage. Once these positive bonds have been established, an act as simple as a kind word or gesture from a trusted adult can release brain chemicals that promote trust, bonding, and empathy, having a significant positive impact on a traumatized child. In this chapter, you'll find helpful information on factors that we as teachers have control over in a school setting that can positively impact students with toxic stress.

Supporting Students Who Are Experiencing Toxic Stress

The *Responsive Classroom* approach to helping students who are experiencing toxic stress is built on six "pillars":

1 Provide an emotionally safe school and classroom

2 Model respectfulness

3 Explicitly teach social and emotional skills

4 Incorporate playfulness into learning

5 Communicate hope

6 Foster your own self-care and build a supportive community

With each of these pillars comes a set of strategies teachers can use in the classroom to build a foundation of support. Combined, these pillars can help you create a safe and healthy environment in which these students can succeed academically and build critical social and emotional skills.

Provide an Emotionally Safe School and Classroom

Developing strong, healthy connections with adults in a predictable school environment can provide a sense of safety that helps reduce the likelihood of students going into fight, flight, or freeze mode. This sense of safety supports a classroom culture where students feel valued and are comfortable taking risks, which can improve students' behavior and academic engagement and contribute to their mental and physical health.

The *Responsive Classroom* practices of Morning Meeting and closing circle are two good ways to build a safe and strong classroom community. Coming together as a group at these predictable times of day offers a comforting routine to students experiencing toxic stress, allowing them to feel a sense of belonging and build connections with you and with their peers. Giving all students in class the chance to express themselves, such as during the sharing component of Morning Meeting, communicates to students that you are interested in hearing what they have to say and sets the stage for children with toxic stress to put their trust in you. Through Morning Meeting, students can make an easier transition into the school day, and through closing circle, students can peacefully reflect on the day and feel more centered before leaving the classroom.

Other ways to allow students time to reflect and relax include quiet time and calming energizers. Quiet time is a brief and purposeful way to provide a peaceful transition between high-energy periods, such as lunch and recess, and more focused periods of learning. Give students 5 to 15 minutes to independently select and complete an activity from a range of approved choices, such as silently writing, drawing, or meditating. Calming energizers (see pages 124–125) can be useful after an especially active lesson or when you sense that students are feeling stressed out or are getting antsy and need a few minutes to collect themselves before moving on with academic content. When used on a regular basis, both quiet time and calming energizers can not only help students manage toxic stress but can help every student stay focused and ready for learning.

Interactive Modeling (see pages 28–31) is another way to create predictability in your classroom. By teaching students how to complete procedures correctly, you are setting clear, understandable expectations for them to follow. These expectations, along with the procedures and routines students learn through Interactive Modeling, allow for a learning environment where students know with certainty what to do and when and how to do it.

In addition to the practices mentioned above, consider the following tips to help you create an environment where students experiencing toxic stress can feel safe and secure and can build a strong, healthy connection with you and with their peers:

- **Be a good listener.** Listen without interrupting, and choose a place for one-on-one conversations that will have minimal distractions and where you and the student can have some privacy, especially if the child is older or more self-conscious. Make yourself available to listen, but let students decide when they're ready to share their feelings with you. Also, remember that children experiencing toxic stress may sometimes need to talk through difficult experiences more than once. Help them make sense of these experiences, or connect them with a counselor or someone else who can.

- **Ask open-ended questions to encourage students to express themselves.** Be open to their thoughts and ideas, and take their concerns seriously. Paraphrase what they say to make sure you understood them correctly and to let them know you heard them. Stay curious and nonjudgmental. For example, instead of asking "Why do you get so angry during group discussions?" try "What are you feeling during group discussions?"

- **Think about what your body language is communicating.** Physically show that you are focused and actively listening to the child by having an open posture, keeping your eyes focused on the child, and nodding.

- **Demonstrate your trustworthiness** by only making promises you can keep and by maintaining a calm, kind demeanor if a student has an outburst.

- **Make the time-out area a comfortable space** that's conducive to helping children calm down, with age-appropriate seating and soothing decorations. Review the procedure for going to time-out (including going on one's own) as frequently as needed for students to be comfortable going.

Connecting With Students

Ms. Meehan, Grade 4 ● Ms. Meehan emphasizes the importance of building bonds with her students—finding out what they like and what they are like. She says that the act of asking what students need is, in itself, a way to build rapport with them and provide reassurance. By fourth grade, she finds that most students either know what they need or are willing to try suggestions, and that making those suggestions shows you care and helps bring down the walls around the student.

Ms. Ghosh, Grade 2 ● After one of her students has regained control following an outburst, Ms. Ghosh likes to talk with them about what they think will help them calm down the next time an incident occurs. It might be going to the time-out area, the student's desk, the buddy teacher's room, or somewhere more customized to that particular student's needs. For instance, one student didn't want others looking at him in the time-out area, so he and Ms. Ghosh agreed that he could sit behind the bookshelf where his classmates couldn't see him when he needed to calm down, as long as Ms. Ghosh could check on him every few minutes.

Mr. Hunter, Grade 5 ● Mr. Hunter strives to give all his students a safe bubble in response to the stressful events of the world, whether those students are experiencing toxic stress or individual difficult events. He recalls one student who was having a tough time because his grandfather was dying. Mr. Hunter met with the student frequently to see how he was doing, talk about ways to use this experience as an opportunity to connect with his grandfather, and share his own personal experiences with loss. On the day his grandfather passed away, the student came to school and shared his news in Morning Meeting, where the rest of the class had the opportunity to offer their condolences and come together as a community. The experience proved that this student knew he could be his true self at school with his classmates and Mr. Hunter, and that he wanted to be there.

To learn more about the practices mentioned in this section, see:

The Morning Meeting Book by Carol Davis and Roxann Kriete (Center for Responsive Schools, 2014)

Closing Circles: 50 Activities for Ending the Day in a Positive Way by Dana Januszka and Kristen Vincent (Center for Responsive Schools, 2012)

Energizers! 88 Quick Movement Activities that Refresh and Refocus by Susan Lattanzi Roser (Center for Responsive Schools, 2009)

Model Respectfulness

Building a climate of respect is important for the success and well-being of all students, but particularly those experiencing toxic stress (Cohen, Cardillo, and Pickeral 2011). Children who experience toxic stress may be more likely than others to interpret innocent interactions as disrespectful, and they may act out when they're feeling disrespected (Tough 2016). Thus, displaying respect toward your students and encouraging them to act respectfully toward one another can help those experiencing toxic stress to feel calmer, more comfortable, and less likely to go into fight, flight, or freeze mode.

True respect goes beyond simple courtesy. In order to feel respected, students need to feel that others are listening to them and taking them seriously. We can act respectfully toward our students by showing curiosity for what they have to say, getting to know them as individuals, and making sure that everyone in the classroom has a voice. We can use the *Responsive Classroom* practice of Academic Choice to allow students to learn in ways that are challenging yet comfortable for them, thereby showing that we respect their autonomy. And we can ensure that we are patient and empathetic when offering help or presenting feedback.

One of the most powerful tools we have for modeling respectfulness is our teacher language. Reinforcing language (see pages 22–23) lets students know what we see them doing well. By reinforcing their strengths, we can deepen our relationships with students and encourage their trust by showing our respect for their skills and efforts. Offering reinforcement also helps students develop confidence in themselves as they witness the things they're doing well, which can help them build their own sense of self-respect.

Reminding language (see pages 23–24) also allows us the opportunity to demonstrate respect for students by showing that we believe in their ability to stay on task and make good choices about their behavior. Because reminding language may be used in response to behavior that's beginning to go off course, it's essential to pay attention to your word choice, tone, and body language when delivering reminders to students experiencing toxic stress. Keep your reminders calm, direct, and focused on the behavior rather than the student, and be sure that you've clearly taught the procedure or behavior you expect the student to demonstrate before using reminding language.

In addition to modeling respectfulness yourself, you can help build a climate of respect in your classroom community by teaching cooperation skills and allowing students ample opportunities to practice. Cooperation skills can help students work together with peers and manage conflicts productively. This is especially important for students experiencing toxic stress, who may find it challenging to connect with others and, as a result, may not have a strong feeling of belonging. Help students build cooperation skills with the following tips:

- **Create opportunities for students to work with their peers toward a common goal.** One of the guiding principles of the *Responsive Classroom* approach is that great cognitive growth occurs through social interaction. Learning to work well with others is especially important for children experiencing toxic stress.

- **Teach and model how groups can work together** to generate possible solutions to a problem, assess those solutions, and choose one to try (for example, through class meetings; see pages 107–109).

- **Help students control their emotions and work through obstacles** so that they can be productive group members. Encourage them to ask for help when needed, share their opinions (including differing opinions) respectfully, and take breaks when they get frustrated or stuck.

- **Identify other sources of support** students may be able to draw on in school and in the community when they need help, such as free counseling services, local support groups, and community advocates.

To learn more about Academic Choice, see *The Joyful Classroom: Practical Ways to Engage and Challenge Students K–6* (Center for Responsive Schools, 2016).

Explicitly Teach Social and Emotional Skills

Since children experiencing toxic stress can easily lose control when their instinctive reaction to go into fight, flight, or freeze mode kicks in, they need help to practice controlling their impulses. Fortunately, the classroom provides ample opportunities for teaching and practicing self-control, which allows students to regulate their thoughts, emotions, and behaviors. Being able to notice what's happening, adjust one's behavior, and transition back to the current task are ways in which students can demonstrate responsibility and accountability in their academic and social lives.

Role-playing (see pages 65–67) is a good way to teach students how to exhibit self-control in both academic and social situations. This technique gives students a safe way to practice what to do in challenging scenarios by using made-up examples at a time when tension is low. Be sure to provide students with adequate opportunities to practice self-control skills, and provide individual support to any students who need additional help. As students try out these skills in real-life scenarios, reinforce their progress.

> The classroom provides ample opportunities for teaching and practicing self-control.

In situations where you see a student beginning to struggle with self-control, use visual and verbal cues and teacher proximity (see pages 68–69) to help the student get back in control of their behavior just as it's beginning to get off task. Using a technique such as increased teacher proximity lets students know that you're paying attention, and it shows that you believe in their ability to meet expectations—thereby helping to build trust between you and the student and encouraging their confidence in their own skills.

If a student continues to struggle with self-control and the situation has escalated to misbehavior, logical consequences (see pages 77–93) may be of help. Although they may not work in every instance for children experiencing toxic stress, logical consequences can often provide needed support when a student has lost control, and can offer a blueprint for what self-control looks like. By having students take a time-out when they need to calm down, guiding them to fix something they've broken, or removing a privilege that isn't being used responsibly, you show them how to get back on task, and you teach students strategies to help them be more successful next time. (If the situation has escalated beyond ordinary misbehavior to the point of being a full-blown outburst, see pages 130–135 for strategies to try.)

As you think about the skills students experiencing toxic stress may need help learning and practicing on the road to self-control, consider the following ideas:

- **Help students talk about their feelings and translate their emotions into words.** If you notice from their facial expression, posture, or other nonverbal signals that they seem sad, angry, or frustrated, help them identify and label those feelings.

- **Help children feel comfortable expressing their emotions** by giving them safe outlets to explore those feelings, such as pretend play, art, or creative writing. Take their feelings and concerns seriously even if those concerns seem minor to you.

- **Work with students to anticipate challenges they may face** in upcoming projects, and generate possible solutions to those challenges together. You can adapt the practice of role-playing (see pages 65–67) for one-on-one use, which is a great technique for coming up with these ideas and testing them out.

- **Teach students problem-solving skills for a variety of situations,** such as finding a way to share materials with a classmate or figuring out a difficult math problem or vocabulary word. Help them work through problems instead of providing the answer. Acknowledge their efforts at solving problems even if those efforts are not completely successful.

- **When children are calm, teach them skills** they can use when their stress begins to rise, such as meditation and relaxation techniques, positive self-talk and affirmations, yoga, and tactile grounding techniques like standing with their back pressed to the wall or running their hands under cold water. Discuss appropriate techniques for using at one's desk, in the time-out space, or in other appropriate areas.

Incorporate Playfulness Into Learning

While the learning students do in the classroom is serious and important work, bringing a spirit of playfulness to that work can help students feel more comfortable, open, and creative. Playfulness thrives when we foster low-risk competition, shared engagement, friendly conversation, and opportunities to be silly.

Play also has an important role in emotional development. Engaging in play can help people reduce stress and become better at coping with it. Since playfulness is malleable—a mood rather than a fixed personality characteristic—we can encourage it in students experiencing toxic stress to help them feel a stronger sense of belonging, significance, and fun and engage more deeply with the learning community. Incorporating playfulness into every element of the school day can help students feel more comfortable in the classroom and more interested in taking part in academics.

In addition to being a brain-based strategy for sustaining academic engagement and encouraging cognitive growth, energizers are an excellent way to incorporate playfulness in the classroom. These fun activities offer students a chance to relax and enjoy themselves and to make connections with you and with their peers. Energizers also help to build the classroom's group identity as you discover those activities the class wants to repeat over and over again. If some students are reluctant to participate, find lower-risk ways to include them, such as by having them turn the lights off during a quiet energizer, point to the words during a song, or simply observe during the activity and then share what they saw. This type of indirect involvement may pave the way for students to feel more comfortable fully participating next time.

In addition to energizer breaks, you can incorporate playfulness at many other points during the school day. As you plan your lessons, consider the following ideas to foster fun and engagement for students experiencing toxic stress:

- **Maintain a sense of humor.** Be willing to laugh at yourself or find the humor in a challenging situation, when appropriate. Also, find the lighthearted side of your academic content by using (or having students create) riddles or jokes that incorporate history facts, scientific terms, or vocabulary words.

- **Encourage creative play** through dress-up, skits, dance, songs, drawings, and other such activities. Try having students create a board game or comic strip about a topic they're studying. Allowing for this type of playful engagement can help all students better engage with academic content.

- **Appeal to students' natural inquisitiveness.** Build excitement by having students follow their own curiosity as they do science experiments, explore the classroom library, grow seeds, or go on nature walks or field trips.

To find more ways to support a fun and engaging classroom, see:

Energizers! 88 Quick Movement Activities That Refresh and Refocus by Susan Lattanzi Roser (Center for Responsive Schools, 2009)

The Joyful Classroom: Practical Ways to Engage and Challenge Students K–6 (Center for Responsive Schools, 2016)

Play has an important role in emotional development.

Communicate Hope

Hope is more than wishful thinking—it is a cognitive process that can be strengthened through learning and practice. According to C. R. Snyder's (1994) theory of hope, this process centers around the pursuit of goals and the belief that one is capable of achieving them. Children who experience the difficulties that result in toxic stress may have a hard time envisioning a positive future for themselves. By recognizing and nurturing their unique talents and showing that you believe in their potential, you can build their sense of hope by helping them picture a future where they can thrive.

Envisioning language (see page 21) is one of the most important ways to help students build their sense of hope. This type of teacher language helps students picture their own future successes, which is the first step toward achieving positive outcomes. These successes may be large and in the distant future, such as a career goal, or smaller and more immediate, such as a classroom project due the following week. Either way, the purpose of envisioning language is the same: to name positive identities and outcomes in order to build students' confidence and help them aim high and meet their goals.

The *Responsive Classroom* practice of Academic Choice offers another method for building students' sense of hope. By providing a set of teacher-guided choices about what to learn, how to learn, or both, we can empower students to get more engaged in what they're learning and to build their own vision for their academic future. Academic Choice offers a supported way to help students develop autonomy and self-confidence through its three stages: planning, working, and reflection.

To learn more about Academic Choice, see *The Joyful Classroom: Practical Ways to Engage and Challenge Students K–6* (Center for Responsive Schools, 2016).

Other tips for helping students build a stronger sense of hope include the following:

- **Help students set short- and long-term goals** and build the skills required to reach them. Break goals and tasks into achievable pieces. When students get stuck, reinforce their efforts to get where they have so far, and help them find ways to move forward.

- **Promote positive risk-taking,** and reinforce that mistakes are a part of learning. Help children reflect on their mistakes and figure out new strategies they can try next time.

- **Nurture students' creativity and curiosity** through the arts and pretend play, exploring their natural environment, and discovering topics that interest them. Talk about the career paths people can take based on these interests. When possible, connect students with afterschool programs or other activities focused on their interests.

- **Use fiction or stories about real people as a springboard** to talk about successful scientists, writers, musicians, doctors, and other role models. Discuss why students look up to their role models and the challenges those role models faced on the road to achieving their goals.

- **Help students see themselves as valuable members of the classroom community** by giving them classroom leadership roles.

- **Talk with students about ways to find friends** who believe in them and with whom they have an authentic connection.

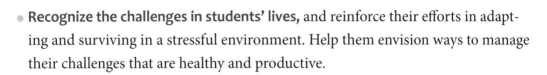

- **Recognize the challenges in students' lives,** and reinforce their efforts in adapting and surviving in a stressful environment. Help them envision ways to manage their challenges that are healthy and productive.

- **Help all students celebrate their accomplishments** and the things that make them unique. Give genuine reinforcing feedback for students' successes, even if they are small. Pay special attention to accomplishments in the areas of taking healthy risks and trying new things, connecting with others, and persevering through challenging situations, as these skills may require extra support for children experiencing toxic stress.

- **Remember and recognize** students' birthdays and other special occasions.

Foster Your Own Self-Care and Build a Supportive Community

As teachers, we give deeply of ourselves to students, and it's easy to lose track of just how much time and energy we've spent until we find ourselves depleted and stressed out. Taking the time for self-care isn't a luxury; it's a necessity not only for our own well-being but for our ability to help our students. Students who are experiencing toxic stress may need a higher than average amount of support, and we may also share in their emotional burden when we empathize with the challenges these students face. Especially if your classroom includes many traumatized students or students who are particularly prone to outbursts, finding support to help you manage your class and your own stress is essential.

A buddy teacher (see pages 87–88) can be a key source of support when you're dealing with misbehavior and outbursts. Because buddy teacher time-out is often an effective option for students who grow self-conscious in regular time-out, it can be useful for students experiencing toxic stress, who may be more prone to self-consciousness. Knowing that a buddy teacher is there for us in difficult moments can help us feel a sense of reassurance that we aren't alone.

It's also important to spend energy not just on helping your students but on tending to your own growth and well-being. If you have experienced trauma in your own life, you may feel especially stressed by seeing what your students are going through. Remember to be patient with yourself just as you would with your students. Like them, you also need time, space, and empathy in order to heal. Even if you haven't experienced a major trauma firsthand, helping students experiencing toxic stress on an ongoing basis can lead to what's known as secondary traumatic stress, also called compassion fatigue or empathic distress (National Child Traumatic Stress Network, n.d.). Warning signs of secondary traumatic stress include guilt, anger, hopelessness, social withdrawal, sleep problems, increased susceptibility to physical ailments, and feelings of disconnection from others. If you are experiencing any of these symptoms, take them seriously. Managing your own stress now can help you avoid burnout, stay healthy, and remain positive about teaching (Changing Minds, n.d.-b).

Consider the following areas to help you take care of your own needs:

- **Pay attention to your emotional health.** In times of stress, take a moment to connect with your own feelings and your body's signals. Learn and practice self-soothing strategies like deep breathing to help you calm down. Also, consider seeking out professional help to work through your feelings. A therapist or counselor can provide a safe, nonjudgmental space for you to vent and talk honestly about what you're going through, which can help you be more present in the classroom and in the rest of your life.

- **Maintain good habits for your physical health.** It's easy to let go of the basics during times of stress, but make a point to eat well, drink enough water, exercise, and get adequate sleep. These essential aspects of a healthy life can help you feel better physically, more balanced emotionally, and better able to focus and stay calm under pressure.

- **Just as you recognize students' successes, celebrate your own—large and small!** Keep a list of the good things you do with students to refer to on difficult days. Regularly complimenting colleagues about what they're doing well can also help you stay in a positive mindset, and it can build a sense of community. You can also turn to your colleagues to work through challenges as a group, discuss self-care strategies, or simply chat and relax together.

- **Think about how you can make your classroom space more welcoming,** not just to students but to yourself as well. Do you have a comfortable chair? Does the room's decor reflect your personality? Think about the room as a whole, as well as any spaces that are yours, such as your desk. You could bring in pictures of family or pets, photographs from places you've traveled, crafts you've made, or framed notes from former students to keep on your desk to help you feel connected to the things that matter most to you.

- **Keep a positive outlook.** Think back on why you became a teacher in the first place. Write a statement or poem about your purpose or create a piece of art to hang in your classroom in order to keep yourself inspired. Think about others who inspire you, too, and make a point to spend time with them.

- **Think about your work-life balance.** Are you making time for your hobbies and interests? How about trying a new creative, athletic, volunteer, or other project that you've always wanted to do?

Take these steps to support yourself because, most importantly, you need and deserve it. But also remember that by prioritizing your own health and well-being, you're setting an important example for students who may have little exposure to what healthy coping mechanisms look like. As always, you are modeling ways for them to behave in the classroom and in the world.

Responding to Outbursts and Withdrawal

A heightened fight, flight, or freeze impulse is a natural adaptation for children who have developed the ability to pick up on subtle signs of danger in order to protect themselves—to know, for example, that the sound of a slammed door means a fight is coming, or to recognize the speech patterns of a parent who has been drinking. Different students dealing with toxic stress will go into fight, flight, or freeze mode in different ways when they are feeling stressed. But whether students have an outburst, escape the situation, or shut down, they are not able to engage with learning in those moments. First and foremost, they need help to calm down and get back in control of themselves.

> First and foremost, children need help to calm down and get back in control of themselves.

In fight mode, students may lash out in a rush to defend themselves against a perceived threat, or they may become defiant with a teacher who they feel is disrespecting them. Other students will go into flight mode, literally fleeing from the situation or even the classroom if they feel threatened. Still others may freeze, becoming overwhelmed by the amount of sensory data taken in when they're under stress and shutting down as a result.

In any of these situations, it's essential to handle the incident with care and compassion. Harsh, punitive approaches, such as suspension, may only exacerbate the situation, as they don't address the student's basic needs. In addition, removing students from school can make them fall behind in their academic work, leading to more frustration and, thus, more outbursts or students' shutting down even more. Mishandling these incidents can also create a tense or uncertain classroom environment where all students feel unsafe. The tips below offer insights on how to handle incidents in a way that is as peaceful, productive, and safe as possible for everyone involved.

Before an Outburst or Other Incident

It's always important to know your students, and when dealing with children who are experiencing toxic stress, knowing students' needs is especially crucial. Learning what factors may lead to an outburst or a student shutting down can help you avoid these situations, and knowing a student's subtle signals that a meltdown is impending can help you manage the situation before it gets out of control.

Through observation, conversations, and spending time with students experiencing toxic stress, we can learn which times and situations are more likely to push students into fight, flight, or freeze mode. We can also discover warning signs that precede a student's loss of self-control, as well as strategies and techniques that help defuse difficult situations. And as we spend time observing all of our students, we can notice which students in the class have a calming effect on individuals experiencing toxic stress.

Some of the strategies in the six pillars outlined earlier in this chapter may be useful to help forestall a potential outburst. When you see something trigger a student's stress response or when you see the warning signs that they may be about to lose control, you might find visual cues, verbal cues, or teacher proximity (see pages 68–69) useful in helping the student reestablish self-control. You might even have a specific signal you use with that particular child, such as a hand on their shoulder or another calming gesture that the two of you have agreed on in advance.

It may also be useful to have the student leave the situation before it becomes overly stressful and sends them into a state of fight, flight, or freeze. You could do this by sending them to time-out, but make sure you've established a consistent habit of using time-out with all students in a nonpunitive way first (see pages 84–87). You might also try sending the student to buddy teacher time-out (see pages 87–88) if they need a little more distance. Or, you might simply send the student on an errand or for a quick walk down the hall and back. Again, knowing what each student needs will help you find the right approach.

Discussing a student's behavior with them won't be productive until after their thinking mind is back in charge.

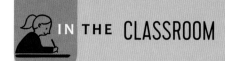

IN THE CLASSROOM

Responding to Outbursts and Withdrawal

Ms. Ghosh, Grade 2   Toxic stress can manifest in different ways: some students may shut down while others may exhibit outbursts. Though it may not be as disruptive to the class as a whole, shutting down, or withdrawal, is just as important to address. Ms. Ghosh remembers one student who was easily embarrassed and who shut down when faced with going to time-out, being helped with math, and many other situations—including talking about what those situations were. Ms. Ghosh found that the best approach was to carefully watch the student to identify his triggers and then find ways to work with him that wouldn't activate those triggers. For instance, when she noticed the student struggling with a math problem, she would use her language very carefully so it didn't sound like criticism: "I see you completed the first three math problems on your own. Would you like help with the fourth?"

Ms. Meehan, Grade 4   Ms. Meehan notes the need for as much patience as possible when a student is having an outburst. She advises taking a break if needed to maintain your composure, and being even calmer than you usually would to compensate for the student's heightened emotions. She thinks of it like drinking a cool glass of milk to soothe your tongue if you've eaten too much hot sauce. The hotter the student's emotions, the cooler and calmer the response should be. She also encourages empathy from the rest of the class toward a child experiencing an outburst. After an incident occurs, she often reminds students that everyone in the class is working on learning self-control, and that everyone needs different things to help them learn. She makes sure to say all this in a kind, understanding tone, and then to promptly move on with the business of the classroom.

Mrs. Badge, Grade K • Always have empathy, advises Mrs. Badge, and never antagonize students or put them on the spot. Building strong relationships with children right from the start helps avoid a lot of problems because it helps her identify and avoid individual students' hot buttons. With children experiencing toxic stress, her radar is always up so she can watch for the early warning signs of an outburst and take steps to prevent it. If an outburst does occur and she needs help managing it, her school has a "smile team" she can call, consisting of the principal, a counselor or social worker, and other trained staff who can come help a child in or out of the classroom.

Mr. Wade, Grade 3 • Many students who regularly have outbursts as a result of toxic stress may expect to be punished, and they may be surprised to be treated with compassion, says Mr. Wade. He tries to think creatively when coming up with logical consequences for these students, and he does his best to incorporate what they tell him they need. Sometimes, he asks a student who's having a hard time, "Is there anyone here you feel comfortable talking to about it?" If so, Mr. Wade privately asks that classmate or adult to spend a few minutes walking and talking with the student who's in distress in order to help them calm down.

Responding to Outbursts in the Moment

When an outburst happens, the most important first step is to regain control of the situation and make sure the student and everyone else in the classroom is safe. This may require moving the student to a new space or distracting them from the situation, whichever works best to help them calm down and feel safe. Each student will have their own unique needs, and knowing those needs can help us respond to the student in the way that's most effective. For example, a student who starts shouting at a classmate during a group project might need to go to time-out or leave the room, or they might simply need to work on something else for a while.

Any conversations about the child's behavior should happen only after the child has calmed down and regained self-control. Neuroscience shows that during moments of stress, the amygdala (the part of the brain focused on survival instincts and emotional memory) can take control over the prefrontal cortex (the "thinking" mind) as stress hormones flood the body (Goleman 1995). Thus, we can't think rationally when we're experiencing a great deal of stress. As a result, discussing a student's behavior with them won't be productive until after their thinking mind is back in charge.

Sending the child to time-out may be appropriate if you haven't done so already. Or, if sending the student to time-out has escalated the incident, now might be the time to send for your buddy teacher (see pages 87–88). You may also need to call on a guidance counselor, principal, or other colleague to take the student someplace where they can calm down, like to the counselor's office, to a designated cool-down or meditation room, or on a walk around the building. Stay in communication with these professionals throughout the school year so that they will be familiar with the child's needs and challenges, and they will be prepared to assist when needed.

Maintaining a calm tone of voice and using as few words as possible is especially important when dealing with outbursts. Focus on listening rather than talking, which will help you gather information and figure out how to assist the student. Staying calm will show both the student and the rest of the class that you're maintaining control, which will help everyone feel that the classroom is a safe place. Make sure that your calm tone is sincere so that students know they can trust your words and actions—if they mistrust your sincerity, they may feel threatened, and their behavior could escalate further. Minimize the number of words you use during outbursts, and you might also consider developing a visual signal for sending students to time-out or to go cool off with some meditation so that you can skip words altogether.

Finally, though it can be challenging, it is essential to maintain empathy for a student who is having a meltdown. Try not to take their outbursts, anger, or insults personally—remember that they are simply trying to protect themselves in the way they know how. Dealing with these incidents as discreetly as possible shows students you respect their privacy, and using language that asks "What's happening?" rather than "What's wrong with you?" helps students feel safer and more understood, ultimately leading to a rapport that may help keep outbursts to a minimum. If you find that you are unable to maintain empathy in the moment of an outburst, it's time to have a buddy teacher, paraprofessional, guidance counselor, or other adult take over for the moment. We, too, sometimes need a moment to cool down and get back in control of ourselves, lest we damage our relationships with our students.

After the Student Has Cooled Down

Once the child has calmed down and regained control, speak to them privately, kindly, and nonjudgmentally about what happened, and ask for their input. Doing so can not only help you better understand the student's triggers and warning signs but also help them learn the essential skill of putting their feelings into words—an ability many students experiencing toxic stress struggle with and need support in developing. Teach them other skills, as well, to help them calm themselves when they feel their emotional temperature start to rise, such as meditation, deep breathing, or focusing on physical sensations to help them feel grounded.

Ask, too, what support the student feels would help them avoid outbursts or shutting down and regain self-control in the future. You can make suggestions and see what the student responds to: "Do you think it might help if you took a couple minutes to write in your journal? If you did a few jumping jacks in the hall? If you had a stuffed animal or a ball to squeeze?" Listen to and respect the child's answers to your suggestions, and elicit their ideas, as well. Also elicit feedback from behavior specialists, social workers, and other experts at your school, along with other teachers who have previously worked with the child and may have additional insights.

Managing the Effects of Toxic Stress

1 Toxic stress is the body's response to extreme and prolonged trauma, and can negatively impact children's health, relationships, and ability to succeed in school.

2 Teachers can mitigate the effects of toxic stress using a six-pillar approach: provide an emotionally safe school and classroom; model respectfulness; explicitly teach social and emotional skills; incorporate playfulness into learning; communicate hope; and foster your own self-care and build a supportive community.

3 To help a student having an outburst or shutting down as a result of toxic stress, teachers should work to identify and avoid triggers, stay calm during incidents, and focus on keeping students safe and helping them calm down.

References

Center on the Developing Child of Harvard University. n.d. "Toxic Stress." Accessed June 13, 2018. https://developingchild.harvard.edu/science/key-concepts/toxic-stress/.

Centers for Disease Control and Prevention. n.d. "Adverse Childhood Experiences." Accessed June 13, 2018. https://www.cdc.gov/violenceprevention/acestudy.

Changing Minds. n.d.-a. "Gestures That Can Heal." Accessed June 13, 2018. https://changing mindsnow.org/healing.

Changing Minds. n.d.-b. "Taking Care of Yourself Helps You Take Care of Children." Accessed June 13, 2018. https://changingmindsnow.org/docs/Taking_Care_of_Yourself.pdf.

Cohen, Jonathan, Richard Cardillo, and Terry Pickeral. 2011. "Creating a Climate of Respect." *Educational Leadership* 69, no.1 (September). http://www.ascd.org/publications/educational-leadership/sept11/vol69/num01/Creating-a-Climate-of-Respect.aspx.

Goleman, Daniel. 1995. *Emotional Intelligence: Why It Can Matter More Than IQ*. New York: Bantam Books.

National Child Traumatic Stress Network. n.d. "Secondary Traumatic Stress." Accessed June 13, 2018. http://www.nctsn.org/resources/topics/secondary-traumatic-stress.

Snyder, C. R. 1994. *The Psychology of Hope: You Can Get There From Here*. New York: Free Press.

Tough, Paul. 2016. *Helping Children Succeed: What Works and Why*. New York: Houghton Mifflin Harcourt.

Addressing Bias in the Classroom

I n her first role as a principal, one elementary school educator found herself getting a lot of discipline referrals for kindergartners who were pretend fighting or roughhousing. Teachers were sending these students to the principal's office with the concern that this behavior was problematic and might be a warning sign of violent tendencies. Yet, a few years later, at the principal's next school, the same behavior among kindergartners barely garnered any attention at all.

Why the difference? The first school was in a lower-income, higher-crime community where almost all of the students were black, and the second was in a more affluent, mostly white neighborhood—and teachers' default assumptions about their students were different in these two settings. Behaviors that were developmentally typical for kindergartners were handled in disparate ways based on a particular student's race and background. While the teachers involved may not have been openly discriminatory, and likely meant no harm, their actions were based in deeply rooted beliefs of which they may not have been aware. And such actions, taken together over time, may have dramatic effects on students' academic and personal trajectories.

Unconscious Bias

No matter how good our intentions, we are all sometimes influenced by beliefs and stereotypes we aren't aware we hold. This phenomenon is called unconscious bias (Dee and Gershenson 2017). It affects everyone, and it is the result of our brain's natural tendency to make quick judgments based on patterns we've learned from our upbringing, popular culture, and the world around us. As a result, our assumptions about and reactions to students' behavior may vary based on their race, gender, or other characteristics unless we work to recognize and change how our hidden beliefs shape our approach to discipline.

Although we cannot control the influences that have shaped these unconscious beliefs or eliminate them completely, it is our responsibility to minimize the effects they have on students (Kirwan Institute 2015). One of the best ways to do so is to get to know each student well. Learning about their interests, family life, and culture can help us gain empathy for them and react to them as unique individuals rather than stereotypical members of a particular group. Talking about hopes and dreams (see pages 43–44), observing students carefully during collaborative learning, and giving them opportunities to share about their lives during Morning Meeting or other activities are all effective ways to learn about the children in your classroom.

> No matter how good our intentions, we are all sometimes influenced by beliefs and stereotypes we aren't aware we hold.

In addition to knowing our students, we also need to know ourselves. By examining our beliefs and behavior, we can begin to recognize our own biases in order to prevent them from undermining the teaching and learning we want to happen in our classrooms. This process takes time, and includes the following steps.

1 **Recognize and accept that we all have unconscious biases.** No matter how open-minded we may be, unconscious bias is a phenomenon that affects everyone. Accepting this fact without getting defensive about it is an important first step toward mitigating the impact of our own biases.

2 **Question yourself and your behaviors.** Take some time each day to reflect on your interactions with students. Consider questions like these to focus your reflections:

- Are my thoughts, expectations, behaviors, and interactions based on objective observation, data, and realistic assessments of all students' strengths and challenges?

- What evidence do I have to support how I am behaving in my classroom and treating individual students?

- When I greet students at the door, do I welcome all students warmly? Does my greeting let all students know that I care about them and am glad to see them today?

- Do I interact with all students using a neutral, calm stance and tone? Or do I shift my stance with certain students (crossing arms across chest, putting hands on hips, moving closer or farther away, etc.)?

- Do I value every student's comments the same by showing interest and making eye contact with them?

- Do I call on all students, or only an eager few?

- What message does my verbal language convey? Do I offer reinforcement to all students? Do I remind and redirect all students?

3 **As you become aware, catch yourself behaving in ways that reflect an unconscious bias.** Pay attention to how students respond to you, and take the opportunity to correct yourself if you realize you may have treated a student unfairly. Also, pay attention to your own feelings. When you feel impatience or frustration setting in, counteract it by calling it out and taking a moment to collect yourself so that you can proceed with working in a positive, intentional manner with the student. Finally, pay attention to your patterns and set reasonable goals for change. Start by focusing on a single behavior you are confident stems from an unconscious bias, and work on reducing it in your practice by a certain amount in a certain time frame. For example, if you find yourself calling on certain students more than others, you might devise a system for ensuring you call on everyone, such as writing names on craft sticks and pulling them out of a jar at random.

4 **Commit to ongoing work on this issue.** Unconscious bias does not disappear or go away. We minimize its impact on us and our students by making a commitment to question, evaluate, and be honest with ourselves. Rather than downplaying or ignoring your assumptions or spontaneous actions, seek clarity by exploring your feelings and actions in greater depth. As you move forward, continue to correct biased behaviors that slip into your practice. Outside the classroom, commit to learning about cultures and people who are different than you in order to broaden your perspective and reduce the impact of deeply ingrained patterns of bias.

Look for support in this ongoing work by turning to fellow educators. You might try getting together with a colleague, your grade or content team, or the whole staff to address unconscious bias and brainstorm ways of lowering its impact within the school. Try pairing up with a colleague and taking turns observing or recording each other in the classroom to assess and give feedback on body language, verbal language, and interactions with students.

> Rather than downplaying or ignoring your assumptions or spontaneous actions, seek clarity by exploring your feelings and actions in greater depth.

One elementary school teacher saw good results from gathering with groups of colleagues and discussing ways in which other people's biases have affected them personally. For example, everyone in the group took turns listing one personal characteristic (such as "I am a tall black man") and one way in which they don't fit a stereotype about that characteristic ("I am not a basketball player"). This activity fostered discussion and helped these colleagues see beyond stereotypes and build empathy for each other and their students.

Stereotype Threat

In addition to changing our own attitudes and behaviors, it's also important to help students see themselves in positive ways. If we don't take steps to address unconscious bias, it can lead to a student experiencing stereotype threat: the tendency to form a self-image based on others' negative perceptions and assumptions, and to act in accordance with those assumptions (Reducing Stereotype Threat, n.d.). For example, an unconscious bias that boys are more prone to misbehavior than girls may lead a teacher to discipline boys more harshly than girls. The boys in the class may internalize this unspoken message and begin to see themselves as troublemakers, and may then act out in accordance with that self-image.

You can help students build a healthy self-image through the use of positive teacher language. Reinforcing language (pages 22–23) can help them see and build on their own strengths, and envisioning language (page 21) can help them imagine and achieve positive outcomes. Also, take some time to assess the décor in your classroom, the books you select for students to read, and the content of your lesson plans. Do all the students in your class get to see people who look like them in those materials? Are those people portrayed positively as competent, successful, and well-rounded individuals, or in negative, stereotypical ways? The images and stories you offer students send as much of a message as your words do.

Activities that allow students to practice self-affirmation can also be helpful in reducing stereotype threat (Cascio et al. 2015). Self-affirmation can help students achieve several different goals, which are listed in the chart at right with a sample activity for each.

Goal	Activity
Help students recognize and affirm their own positive attributes.	**I Am**—Have students name three to five positive adjectives to describe themselves, for example, "friendly," "thoughtful," "determined," and "brave." Then, have them draw a picture or write a story that shows them acting out these characteristics.
Provide examples of positive role models across diverse demographic groups.	**I Can**—Have students identify someone they admire from a demographic group they belong to. This could be a community leader, an educator, or someone else who has achieved success in their field. Then, have students identify three positive characteristics about that person. Students can draw or write about how they, too, might become a role model in the future.
Build resilience in the face of adversity.	**I Will**—Share ways that prominent role models have overcome adversity on the road to success, and give examples from your own life, too. With these stories fresh in students' minds, use open-ended questions to help students generate ideas about how to overcome the challenges in their lives and see themselves as capable of facing those challenges.
Foster a growth mindset.	**I Learn**—Help students see that intelligence and abilities are not fixed but can be developed and strengthened with time and practice. Share examples of successful individuals in a variety of careers, and discuss the types of skills those people needed to learn and practice in order to achieve success. Also, ask students about their own skills, and have them reflect on the process of building those skills through practice and learning from mistakes.

In conjunction with the guidelines in Chapter 3—such as assuming good intentions, having empathy, and maintaining a spirit of curiosity—the techniques in this appendix can help you ensure fairer discipline for all students in your classroom. As with all the practices in this book, changing one's behavior takes time. Be patient with yourself as you acknowledge and observe your own biases, and have colleagues support you by observing you in action and offering feedback to help you improve. Remember, this is ongoing work, and the goal is to aim for realistic improvement rather than perfection.

References

Cascio, Christopher N., Matthew Brook O'Donnell, Francis J. Tinney, Matthew D. Lieberman, Shelley E. Taylor, Victor J. Strecher, and Emily B. Falk. 2016. "Self-Affirmation Activates Brain Systems Associated With Self-Related Processing and Reward and Is Reinforced by Future Orientation." *Social Cognitive and Affective Neuroscience* 11, no. 4 (April): 621–629. https://doi.org/10.1093/scan/nsv136.

Dee, Thomas and Seth Gershenson. 2017. "Unconscious Bias in the Classroom: Evidence and Opportunities." *Google's Computer Science Education Research.*

Kirwan Institute. n.d. "Strategies for Addressing Implicit Bias in Early Childhood Education." Accessed July 9, 2018. http://kirwaninstitute.osu.edu/wp-content/uploads/2015/06/implicit-bias-strategies.pdf.

Reducing Stereotype Threat. n.d. "What Is Stereotype Threat?" Accessed July 9, 2018. http://www.reducingstereotypethreat.org/what-is-stereotype-threat-2/.

Books to Use
in the Classroom

T he contributors to this book recommend the following children's books as discussion-starters and tools for fostering academic and social-emotional learning.

Picture Books

Agate: What Good is a Moose? by Joy Morgan Dey, illustrated by Nikki Johnson

Alexander and the Terrible, Horrible, No Good, Very Bad Day by Judith Viorst, illustrated by Ray Cruz

Amazing Grace by Mary Hoffman, illustrated by Caroline Binch

Can I Play Too? by Mo Willems

Casey at the Bat by Ernest Lawrence Thayer, illustrated by Barry Moser

Chester's Way by Kevin Henkes

Chrysanthemum by Kevin Henkes

Corduroy by Don Freeman

Dex: the Heart of a Hero by Caralyn Buehner, illustrated by Mark Buehner

Picture Books, continued

The Dot by Peter H. Reynolds

Dream Big, Little Pig! by Kristi Yamaguchi, illustrated by Tim Bowers

Each Kindness by Jacqueline Woodson, illustrated by E. B. Lewis

Enemy Pie by Derek Munson, illustrated by Tara Calahan King

The Flower Man by Mark Ludy

Ish by Peter H. Reynolds

Lilly's Purple Plastic Purse by Kevin Henkes

Me . . . Jane by Patrick McDonnell

Mr. Peabody's Apples by Madonna, illustrated by Loren Long

My Mouth Is a Volcano by Julia Cook, illustrated by Carrie Hartman

My Name Is Not Alexander: Just How Big Can a Little Kid Dream?
    by Jennifer Fosberry, illustrated by Mike Litwin

My Name Is Not Isabella: Just How Big Can a Little Girl Dream? by Jennifer Fosberry,
    illustrated by Mike Litwin

Nobody Owns the Sky: The Story of "Brave Bessie" Coleman by Reeve Lindbergh,
    illustrated by Pamela Paparone

Odd Velvet by Mary E. Whitcomb, illustrated by Tara Calahan King

Of Thee I Sing: A Letter to My Daughters by Barack Obama, illustrated by Loren Long

One by Kathryn Otoshi

The Other Side by Jacqueline Woodson, illustrated by E. B. Lewis

A Quiet Place by Douglas Wood, illustrated by Dan Andreasen

The Recess Queen by Alexis O'Neill, illustrated by Laura Huliska-Beith

Sandwich Swap by Kelly DiPucchio and Queen Rania Al-Abdullah,
    illustrated by Tricia Tusa

The Sneetches and Other Stories by Dr. Seuss

Strega Nona by Tomie dePaola

Thank You, Mr. Falker by Patricia Polacco

Two by Kathryn Otoshi

Wemberly Worried by Kevin Henkes

When Sophie Gets Angry—Really, Really Angry by Molly Bang

When Sophie's Feelings Are Really, Really Hurt by Molly Bang

Wilma Unlimited: How Wilma Rudolph Became the World's Fastest Woman
    by Kathleen Krull, illustrated by David Diaz

The Velveteen Rabbit by Margery Williams

Zero by Kathryn Otoshi

Chapter Books

Al Capone Does My Shirts by Gennifer Choldenko

Because of Winn-Dixie by Kate DiCamillo

Charlotte's Web by E. B. White, illustrated by Garth Williams

Crenshaw by Katherine Applegate

The Lemonade War by Jacqueline Davies

The Lions of Little Rock by Kristin Levine

Marley: A Dog Like No Other by John Grogan

Matilda by Roald Dahl, illustrated by Quentin Blake

The Miraculous Journey of Edward Tulane by Kate DiCamillo,
    illustrated by Bagram Ibatoulline

The One and Only Ivan by Katherine Applegate, illustrated by Patricia Castelao

Out of My Mind by Sharon M. Draper

Wonder by R. J. Palacio

Further Resources

All of the recommended practices in this book come from or are consistent with the *Responsive Classroom* approach to teaching—an evidence-based education approach associated with greater teacher effectiveness, higher student achievement, and improved school climate. *Responsive Classroom* practices help educators build competencies in four interrelated domains: engaging academics, positive community, effective management, and developmentally responsive teaching.

To learn more about the *Responsive Classroom* approach, see the following resources published by Center for Responsive Schools and available from www.responsiveclassroom.org.

Classroom Management: Set up and run a classroom in ways that enable the best possible teaching and learning.

Interactive Modeling: A Powerful Technique for Teaching Children by Margaret Berry Wilson. 2012.

What Every Teacher Needs to Know, K–5 series, by Margaret Berry Wilson and Mike Anderson. 2010–2011.

Teaching Children to Care: Classroom Management for Ethical and Academic Growth K–8, revised ed., by Ruth Sidney Charney. 2002.

Morning Meeting: Gather as a whole class each morning to greet each other, share news, and warm up for the day of learning ahead.

The Morning Meeting Book, 3rd ed., by Roxann Kriete and Carol Davis. 2014.

80 Morning Meeting Ideas for Grades K–2 by Susan Lattanzi Roser. 2012.

80 Morning Meeting Ideas for Grades 3–6 by Carol Davis. 2012.

Doing Math in Morning Meeting: 150 Quick Activities That Connect to Your Curriculum by Andy Dousis and Margaret Berry Wilson. 2010. (Includes a Common Core State Standards correlation guide.)

Doing Science in Morning Meeting: 150 Quick Activities That Connect to Your Curriculum by Lara Webb and Margaret Berry Wilson. 2013. (Includes correlation guides to the Next Generation Science Standards and *A Framework for K–12 Science Education,* the basis for the standards.)

Doing Language Arts in Morning Meeting: 150 Quick Activities That Connect to Your Curriculum by Jodie Luongo, Joan Riordan, and Kate Umstatter. 2015. (Includes a Common Core State Standards correlation guide.)

Doing Social Studies in Morning Meeting: 150 Quick Activities That Connect to Your Curriculum by Leah Carson and Jane Cofie. 2017. (Includes correlation guides to the National Curriculum Standards for Social Studies—The Themes of Social Studies, the *College, Career, & Civic Life C3 Framework for Social Studies State Standards,* and the Common Core State Standards for English Language Arts.)

Positive Teacher Language: Use words and tone as a tool to promote students' active learning, sense of community, and self-discipline.

The Power of Our Words: Teacher Language That Helps Children Learn, 2nd ed., by Paula Denton, EdD. 2014.

Teacher Language for Engaged Learning: 4 Video Study Sessions. 2013.

Engaging Academics: Learn tools for effective teaching and making lessons lively, appropriately challenging, and purposeful to help students develop higher levels of motivation, persistence, and mastery of skills and content.

The Joyful Classroom: Practical Ways to Engage and Challenge Students K–6. From *Responsive Classroom.* 2016.

The Language of Learning: Teaching Students Core Thinking, Speaking, and Listening Skills by Margaret Berry Wilson. 2014.

Teaching Discipline: Use practical strategies, such as rule creation and positive responses to misbehavior, to promote self-discipline in students and build a safe, calm, and respectful school climate.

Teasing, Tattling, Defiance and More: Positive Approaches to 10 Common Classroom Behaviors by Margaret Berry Wilson. 2013.

Responsive School Discipline: Essentials for Elementary School Leaders by Chip Wood and Babs Freeman-Loftis. 2011.

Foundation-Setting During the First Weeks of School: Take time in the critical first weeks of school to establish expectations, routines, a sense of community, and a positive classroom tone.

The First Six Weeks of School, 2nd ed. From *Responsive Classroom.* 2015.

Movement, Games, Songs, and Chants: Sprinkle quick, lively activities throughout the school day to keep students energized, engaged, and alert.

Closing Circles: 50 Activities for Ending the Day in a Positive Way by Dana Januszka and Kristen Vincent. 2012.

Energizers! 88 Quick Movement Activities That Refresh and Refocus by Susan Lattanzi Roser. 2009.

99 Activities and Greetings: Great for Morning Meeting . . . and Other Meetings, Too! by Melissa Correa-Connolly. 2004.

Preventing Bullying at School: Use practical strategies throughout the day to create a safe, kind environment in which bullying is far less likely to take root.

How to Bullyproof Your Classroom by Caltha Crowe. 2012. (Includes bullying prevention lessons.)

Solving Behavior Problems With Children: Engage students in solving their behavior problems so they feel safe, challenged, and invested in changing.

Sammy and His Behavior Problems: Stories and Strategies from a Teacher's Year by Caltha Crowe. 2010.

Solving Thorny Behavior Problems: How Teachers and Students Can Work Together by Caltha Crowe. 2009.

Child Development: Understand children's common physical, social-emotional, cognitive, and language characteristics at each age, and adapt teaching to respond to children's developmental needs.

Yardsticks: Child and Adolescent Development Ages 4–14, 4th ed., by Chip Wood. 2017.

Yardsticks Guide Series: Common Developmental Characteristics in the Classroom and at Home, Grades K–8 (based on *Yardsticks* by Chip Wood). From *Responsive Classroom*. 2018.

Special Area Educators: Explore key *Responsive Classroom* practices adapted for a wide variety of special areas.

Responsive Classroom for Music, Art, PE, and Other Special Areas. From *Responsive Classroom*. 2016.

Professional Development/Staff Meetings: Learn easy-to-use structures for getting the most out of your work with colleagues.

Energize Your Meetings! 35 Interactive Learning Structures for Educators. From *Responsive Classroom*. 2014.

Publisher's Acknowledgments

Center for Responsive Schools wishes to thank Laurie Badge, Suzy Ghosh, Earl Hunter II, Caitie Meehan, and Cory Wade for enriching this book by sharing their stories and their expertise. Thanks also to Jane Cofie and Karen Poplawski for adding their thoughts and experiences to the conversation.

More than thirty years in the making, the *Responsive Classroom* approach to teaching continues to evolve thanks to the thousands of educators whose hard work and dedication improves students' lives all around the world. Our gratitude goes out to everyone who undertakes this essential work.